MISUNDERSTOOD

The Life and Legacy of Joseph

Laura Ford

Quick question, Dear Friend...

Have you ever wondered how we have made it this far? By that, I mean, when we look at our lives it seems surreal that through all the twists and turns, we are where we are today. Do you feel that way sometimes? As I sit here, I consider the mercy of God in the very breath I breathe and think, "Why would He choose to redeem and seek a relationship with those who have done nothing but push Him away and doubt Him at every turn?" What a merciful, loving Father! No earthly father can ever compare to our Heavenly Father. Take heart, dear friend, if your father has let you down. The very God who created you sees you as His daughter and His prized possession. He most certainly will not let you down!

If only I could look into your eyes and tell you face to face how excited I am you have opened the pages of this study and quite possibly purposed in your heart to see it through to the end! I love how God uses men and women of the Bible to stir our hearts with a holy passion for His presence and holiness in our lives. Just think of this study as the ladle we will use to dip into the deep waters of life found within the Scriptures, drawing them out to hydrate our souls! You may be approaching this study with a supreme knowledge of God's precious Word or you may be already terrified to keep reading. Let me tell you so plainly that if I can study the Bible and have the God of all Heaven and earth speak to me through it, He most assuredly will speak to you, my sister!

Do not be afraid to open wide your heart and soul, letting Jesus see all that is hidden within. He desires to heal you and restore you completely but long before that can begin, He must have all of you. Everything you are must be His because He is not one to settle for second best. There was no wisdom to be found in my life until repentance and salvation became the sole purpose of why I exist in the first place.

If you have not placed your faith in Jesus Christ, I pray today is the day. However, over the next six weeks, if you are still pondering, processing, and praying for a revelation, let it be that the Messiah opens the very eyes of your heart and shows Himself as the true Lord over all things that ever existed....including you. I love you even though we have never met and pray that one day we will both sit at the feet of the Savior of the world and be speechless.

Much Love, Laura

CONTENTS

I dedicate this study to my two precious daughters, Kate and Lily Beth. You are my full-time calling. My energy, my devotion, and my love are given fully to you. I thank God for accomplishing His will in our very full lives and showing Himself to us from the maddening and mundane, to the most momentous moments of our days!

Every day spent with the two of you is a gift. Your mommy loves you.

A more intriguing story than that of Joseph was never written. What makes it the more wonderful is that it is true.
–Sidlow Baxter[1]

[1] Baxter, J. Sidlow. *Explore the Book*, pg. 60. Zondervan, Grand Rapids, MI: 1960.

INTRODUCTION
Theology by Typology

Studied with good sense and careful eye to New Testament teaching, the typology of the Old Testament is a priceless treasure–mine to the Bible student, and should on no account be neglected. –Baxter[2]

I. What is typology?

–"...they are a form of ________________, fore–picturing persons and things which were yet to be and revealing Divine anticipation of future events."[3]
–"...the typology of the Old Testament furnishes a grand proof of its Divine inspiration."[4]

II. Typology as prophecy, reminds us of the ____________________ of Scripture.

–The life of Joseph is not a mere story, but rather an account of a real boy, becoming a real man and exhibiting a real faith under extreme opposition.

III. Abraham, Isaac, Jacob, and Joseph are known as the great ___________________ of the Old Testament.

–"Patriarch" –the male head of a family or tribe.

IV. Spiritual Characteristics of the Patriarchs, according to Sidlow.

Abraham:
(Hebrews 11:8-12)

Isaac:
(Hebrews 11:17-19)

Jacob:
(Genesis 29)

Joseph:
(Genesis 39-50)

---

[2] Baxter, J. Sidlow. *Explore the Book*, pg. 55. Zondervan, Grand Rapids, MI: 1960.
[3] Ibid
[4] Ibid

GROUP DISCUSSION QUESTIONS:

Theology by Typology

1. How can studying typologies in the Old Testament enhance our understanding of the New Testament?

2. Which typology characteristic of the Patriarchs intrigues you the most?

3. Discuss some of the ways you have seen the characteristics of the Patriarchs lived out in your own life; characteristics of a life of faith, a life of daughter-ship, a life of service, a life of suffering and glory.

4. What do you hope to gain over the next five weeks in studying the life of Joseph?

WEEK ONE:
Family Ties, Family Lies

Day One: Father and Mothers

The family tree is about as complex as the one that may be right outside in your front yard. We could study the scientific inner-workings of every part, along with the growing and dying process and still marvel and the complexity of each species we call the common tree. I am no scientist or environmentalist, so I will not toy with the analogy of a tree much longer, I assure you! Nevertheless, know for certain that you are not alone if the roots of your family pine are about as twisted and mingled below the surface as the one towering beside it. You may have grown up in the most wonderful, loving family in the world or you may still be wishing the nurse had switched your wristband with another baby in the hospital after your mother delivered you! No matter the case, our family has a huge impact on whom and what we become. Thank the Lord we have a redeeming, Heavenly Father who can take even the worst upbringing and use it for His glory. I tread lightly here if I am already tugging at your heartstrings, my sweet sister. Families harbor love–hate relationships and wounds go very deep. Rest assured, you are right where you need to be since the very man whose life we will invade for the next five weeks emerges as the perfect example of showing grace to family members less than deserving.

Now Laban had two daughters; the name of the older was Leah, and the name of the younger was Rachel. Leah had weak eyes, but Rachel had a lovely figure and was beautiful.
Genesis 29:16-17

Yet before we give too much away on our first day of homework, let's meet Joseph's father and mothers. The plural moms will make sense in a few minutes.

Read Genesis 29:16-30 in your Bible and jot down the name of Joseph's father and mothers.

If you have not read this account in Scripture before, you were probably thinking what I was thinking, "Wow, this dysfunctional family to be is off to a great start!" It gets even better. The man in charge of the wedding arrangements was actually Jacob's uncle. So far Jacob had not had the best of luck in his life, even up to his complex relationship with his uncle and two female cousin fiancés. Since it was customary to intermarry with extended family in the time of the Old Testament, Jacob was actually blessed by God to have found this very family after his long journey, having run away from home. His running from home is a story in itself but since we want to briefly highlight Jacob in order to understand Joseph's biography, we will merely hit the highlights of his life throughout our study. Jacob was a major figure, as most fathers are, in the life of his son. So do not fear we are definitely not finished with him yet!

Jacob made love to Rachel also, and his love for Rachel was greater than his love for Leah. And he worked for Laban another seven years.
Genesis 29:30

Although Jacob was forced to marry both Rachel and Leah, who did he love more, according to Genesis 29:30?

No matter how many times I read this story, I do not think it will ever get old to me and I also do not think I will ever get over feeling sorry for Leah. Compared to Rachel, she seemed to linger in the shadows of her younger sister.

How does Genesis 29:16-17 describe the appearance of these two sisters?

How fortunate we are that this is a women's study and that you and I can fully relate to what it feels like to be compared to another woman! Verse 17 describes Leah's eyes as, "weak or tender," meaning she was not as bright eyed or possibly had as bold of features as her younger sis. Other verses in Scripture use this word to describe tender children or even cattle or young calves.[5] I have heard pastors call Leah a cow face but I think that is a bit harsh since the word denotes one who is shy, gentle, or timid. I think we have all felt inferior to another woman at some point in our lives. It can either be our sister, another family relative, best friend, or a woman who we may think is either prettier, smarter, or more out-going and therefore we compare ourselves to them. Has there been any woman or women in your life that you have struggled comparing yourself with?

Who comes to your mind this very moment?

Just the name could potentially conjure a myriad of emotions. Don't worry, the last thing I want to do is get us in a tiff over our other female relationships. However, if we have lived our lives in the shadows of another woman, whoever it may be, I think it's time we come out and see the light! Part of the dysfunction in our relationships stems for our own mindset. Somewhere along life's challenging journey, we gave ourselves permission to be measured up against one or more individuals and let that very comparison thrust us into the shadows of our own insecurity. Not to mention that we subconsciously blame God for not making us just like them or better!

...but let your adorning be the hidden person of the heart with the imperishable beauty of a gentle and quiet spirit, which in God's sight is very precious. 1 Peter 3:4 ESV

In light of 1 Peter 3:4, how can knowing and believing what God considers of great worth and value in a woman help you emerge from the shadows of superficiality?

Instead of hiding in the shadows of what could very well be a wonderful woman of God, I truly believe the Lord would have us more focused on the hidden person of the heart. We do not have to reject or dislike those whom we have either idolized or harbored jealously for in order to no longer be defined by them. In fact, we would be able to love them more genuinely by releasing them and being more concerned with the very thing which God is calling us to cultivate by the power of the Holy Spirit in our lives. And that very thing is a gentle and quiet spirit.

When the LORD saw that Leah was not loved, he enabled her to conceive, but Rachel remained childless. Genesis 29:31

Of course, in matters of the heart, things are easier said than done. As we will see with Leah, being compared to her younger sister would to be the least of her problems now that she was married to a man who didn't love her.

Who else noticed that Leah was not loved by Jacob (Genesis 29:31)?

*She gave this name to the Lord who spoke to her: "You are the God who **sees me**,' for she said, I have now seen the One who sees me." Genesis 16:13*

Reading that the Lord saw Leah was not loved just makes me want to cry. Did I not tell you that we have a loving, intimate Heavenly Father! Leah's father used deception to arrange a marriage for his daughter, but here we see the Lord use none other than sheer compassion and miraculous power to begin restoring His daughter, Leah's, broken heart.

*The Lord has **heard my cry** for mercy; the Lord accepts my prayer. Psalm 6:9*

Do you ever feel as though God is not concerned with the broken condition of your heart or that you have been greatly disappointed in life?

*Cast all your anxiety on Him because **He cares** for you. 1 Peter 5:7*

Sometimes we seem to be missing major pieces that would aid in holding our heart together. It may be the missing piece of a parent, a spouse, a child, an unfulfilled dream,

[5] "Hebrew Lexicon :: H7390 (KJV)." Blue Letter Bible. Sowing Circle. Web. 9 Nov, 2015.

a gross misunderstanding never settled, or anything that you may have lost or never fully possessed in the first place. Whatever it is, you feel its void. Many years may have passed and it may still feel as though God has yet to take notice of you. Let me reassure you, He knows. He sees, He hears, and He cares. How do I know this? His Word promises it. If we only had life's experiences to dictate God's character, we would be horribly disappointed and probably think God was the complete opposite of who He really is. Thank the Lord, we have His sustaining, all-powerful Word to remind us that no matter what is missing in our lives, our Father knows and He cares. Ask the Lord right now to help you believe this, especially in those times where your feelings beg you to think otherwise.

She conceived again, and when she gave birth to a son she said, "This time I will praise the Lord." So she named him Judah. Then she stopped having children. Genesis 29:35

God saw Leah was not loved and therefore He chose to open her womb so that she could have children. Now surely Jacob would love her after she bore him a son, right? Wrong.

How does Leah's response to her fourth son differ from the first three in Genesis 29:32-35?

After Rueben, Simeon, and Levi, comes Judah. Instead of continuing to focus her attention on the one who did not love her, she finally praises the One who does! "This time I will praise the Lord" (Genesis 29:35)!

How could our quest to gain one's affection and attention be misleading?

Though you have not seen Him, you love Him; and even though you do not see Him now, you believe in Him and are filled with an inexpressible and glorious joy, for you are receiving the goal of your faith, the salvation of your souls. 1 Peter 1:8-9

A loving, mutual relationship is a gift. If you currently have a relationship like that, please do not take it for granted. So many women, and you may be one, my dear friend, have broken marriages or no marriage at all. You may be in a marriage right now and you do not feel loved. Or you may feel as though there is not a man in this world who will ever love you with a Christ–like love and if he happens to exist, there is no way he is going to find you! While God desires for our current husbands or future husbands to genuinely love us, He knows we long for a deeper, more satisfying affection that only He can satisfy. We long for an intimacy that transcends anything in the physical or earthly realm. We long for a secure relationship that will last for eternity. We long for Jesus.

Leah finally realized that what was bringing her joy and showering her with favor was the One who could love her more than Jacob ever could! And because she believed that it was the Lord who looked upon her with favor, she was able to exclaim with an inexpressible joy, "This time I will praise the Lord!"

As we close today's homework, take a moment to thank the Lord for the family He has given you. There may be some missing pieces, but even if you only have a close friend who loves you like family, praise the Lord or him or her. Ponder the ways your Heavenly Father has shown you His love and if you still are seeking after it, ask the Lord to make that love known to you in a very real and intimate way throughout our time together. Words cannot express how thankful I am that you would allow me the privilege to study with you. I love you dearly.

Day Two: "Give Me Children, Or I'll Die!"

Yesterday we had our introduction with Joseph's dysfunctional family. I am so very thankful that I do not have to share my husband with my sister! I can't fathom what our household would be like. Someone would have to hide the knives! Now I will say that if my sister and I lived together, we could at least share clothes and shoes, but that would be about the extent of our sharing personal belongings, husbands would definitely not be included in that! I honestly believe that Rachel and Leah were not so hot about having to share Jacob, but unfortunately they were given no say in the matter. However, from what we gathered in yesterday's homework, they seem to have had many of the same struggles that any woman in our generation would have had if placed in the same situation. Our study today will only serve to further validate my point.

As you recall, we left Leah yesterday after the birth of her fourth, precious son, Judah. Now let's see how Rachel responds to her sister's new identity as fertile myrtle momma. While Leah was growing in her faith and praising the Lord for her four beautiful boys, her sister Rachel was seething with jealous anger. My how the tables have turned! Now it's Jacob who needs to hide the knives in their house! Notice how Rachel blamed Jacob. Our poor husbands, it seems that once they say "I do," anything that goes wrong from that point on is their fault. A friend of my husband gave him some very sound advice by telling him, "You can be right or you be happy, but you can't be both." I imagine Jacob, who only desired to have one wife in the first place, was now stuck with the weighty responsibility to make not only one wife, but two wives, happy. You know he must have had moments where celibacy sounded like a beautiful thing! My husband married me later in his life and would often get asked why he stayed single for so long without actively dating to find a wife sooner. His response was often Proverbs 21:9, "Better to live in a desert than with a quarrelsome and ill–tempered wife." Now I will say that he still has to put up with my ill–temper some days, but at least he prayed long and hard that whomever he married would at least be worth putting up with! But poor Jacob! He had both! He lived in a desert and still had not only one, but two quarrelsome and often ill–tempered wives!

When Rachel saw that she was not bearing Jacob any children, she became jealous of her sister. So she said to Jacob, "Give me children, or I'll die!" Genesis 30:1

Better to live in a desert than with a quarrelsome and ill-tempered wife. Proverbs 21:9

As humorous as Proverbs 21:9 can be, it can also be very convicting. Have you found yourself, like me, maybe giving into an ill–temper more often than you ought to?

For the last two months I have been homeschooling our daughters who are six and four years old. Needless to say, I have become, more often than I would like to admit, quite ill–tempered. This transition has brought out the best and worst in me! My husband, Sonny, has had to come home some evenings from work to a wife in tears, daughters sitting in time out, and no dinner on the table or even on the stove for that matter. I promise you I am not an anti–public school mom, so please do not put down your pen and shut your Bible and come to the conclusion that I am crazy...well, that may be debatable at this point, but nonetheless, I am honestly doing what I feel God has called me to do. I firmly believe that some families were meant to homeschool and some were meant to go have their children go to public, private, hybrid, or whatever else. No matter what kind of schooling you are considering for your children or have already seen them through, (or you may not have any children at all and are therefore neutral) God works

through it all! Despite my firm decision and even calling to homeschool, it has still been a struggle! The Lord has been working so gently with my heart by encouraging me through His Word and using godly women who are way more experienced than I to come alongside me and cheer me on. No matter what season you find yourself in, Romans 5:15 is a keeper when it comes to us seeking to live in complete harmony with those closest to us.

Jacob became angry with her and said, "Am I in the place of God, who has kept you from having children?" Genesis 30:2

> *May God who gives patience, steadiness, and encouragement help you to live in complete harmony with each other—each with the attitude of Christ toward the other. Romans 5:15*

Then she said, "Here is my servant Bilhah. Sleep with her so that she can bear children for me and that through her I too can build a family." Genesis 30:3

If any family needed to be in harmony, it was Jacob's.

How did Jacob respond to Rachel after her emotional suicidal threat (Gen 30:2)?

Jacob was probably a little put out at this point with his two sister wives and their constant competitive nature! He must have just thrown his hands up in the air when he replied, "Am I in the place of God, who has kept you from having children?"

Well, if it was God who kept Rachel from having children, how did Rachel plan to manipulate the situation to fit her immediate desire? (Gen 30:3-7)

Poor Bilhah, she probably thought, "What have I gotten myself into?!" Her name in Hebrew is descriptive of a woman who is "timid" or even "troubled."[6] I don't know of anything worse than being right in the middle of a family feud when it's not even your own family! Although, once Bilhah bore a son, Rachel was quite content and even thought for awhile that she had won the battle of the babies. "Then Rachel said, 'I have had a great struggle with my sister, and I have won" (Gen 30:8).

Isn't it funny how the Lord has to get us away from those who have a tendency to give into our every whim and want in order for Him to discipline us and teach us humility and dependency?

Do you know anyone who has a chronic competitive nature?

Some people come by it rather naturally or grew up having to fight to be seen or heard. It may even be that you, my dear sister, see life through a competitive lens. Rachel may have been used to having things her way as often as she pleased under her father's roof. Isn't it funny how the Lord has to get us away from those who have a tendency to give into our every whim and want in order for Him to discipline us and teach us humility and dependency? Even though Rachel, Leah, and Jacob were still living with Laban at this point, life had a way of bringing circumstances that even daddy couldn't fix.

Do you think Rachel did the right thing by giving her servant Bilhah to Jacob?

[6] "H1090-Bilhah (KJV): Strong's Hebrew Lexicon." Blue Letter Bible. Web. 29 March. 2016

Despite Rachel's plan to take matters into her own hands, God still blessed Jacob with twelve sons, representing the twelve tribes of Israel (see Gen 35:23-26). However, when we take circumstances into our own hands, we potentially run the risk of veering outside the boundaries of God's will and having to face the consequences of our actions.

As I was reading one of my favorite devotionals this morning, the message for today spoke precisely of the temptation of trying to take matters into our own hands rather than leave them to the Lord. To say it was a convicting read would be an understatement.

However, when we take circumstances into our own hands, we potentially run the risk of veering outside the boundaries of God's will and having to face the consequences of our actions.

> *Beloved, never try to get out of a dark place except in God's timing and in His way. A time of trouble and darkness is meant to teach you lessons you desperately need. Premature deliverance may circumvent God's work of grace in your life. Commit the entire situation to Him, and be willing to abide in darkness, knowing He is present. Stop interfering with God's plan and with His will. Touching anything of His mars the work. Moving the hands of a clock to suit you does not change the time. You may be able to rush the unfolding of some aspects of God's will, but you will harm His work in the long run. You can force a rosebud open, but you spoil the flower. Leave everything to Him, without exception. "Not what I will, but what You will" (Mark 14:36).*[7]

How do the truths found within this quote speak to you in your current circumstances?

One of the most difficult things for anyone to do is *wait*!

One of the most difficult things for anyone to do is *wait*! Yet we are told over and over again in Scripture that waiting honors God. Of the following verses below, circle one to commit to memory. Even if you are not currently waiting on the Lord for something, it is likely that you will come to that place again and need at least one of these verses as a reminder!

...it is good to wait quietly for the salvation of the Lord.
Lamentations 3:26

But if we hope for what we do not yet have, we wait for it patiently.
Romans 8:25

Though it linger, wait for it; it will certainly come and will not delay.
Habakkuk 3:2

I wait for the Lord, my whole being waits, and in His word I put my hope.
Psalm 130:5

Sometimes I think we try to wait on the Lord with our intellect or even with a portion of our hearts but what a peace that we would receive if we waited upon the Lord with our whole being!

These verses have ministered so deeply to me in times of waiting and I pray they will do the same for you. I especially love how the last verse, Psalm 130:5, says, "...my whole being waits!" Sometimes I think we try to wait on the Lord with our intellect or even with a portion of our hearts but what peace we would receive if we wait upon the Lord with our whole being! That would require a huge measure of dependency on God alone to see us through to the other side of whatever it is we are waiting on. I believe this is exactly how God wants us to live our lives in total and complete dependence on Him. Rachel and Leah sought out the customs of the day in order to justify sharing motherhood with their maidservants. Although God continued to be faithful in the lives of His people, I can't help but wonder what God's best would have been if they had chosen to wait instead of worry. I know I desire God's best, my friend, and I would bet you do as

[7] Cowman, L.B. *Streams In the Desert.*, pg 93-94. Zondervan, Grand Rapids, MI: 1997.

well. Let's pray that we can be women that truly desire to wait on the Lord with our whole beings!

Day Three: The Brother's Grim Intrigue

I promise you that we will get around to studying the very man whom this study is written about, but we just can't introduce him and all the chaos that surrounded his life without further investigating his, let's say, rather complicated family!

I would be tickled beyond belief if you sat down to this study having never read the Biblical account of Joseph!

Joseph's brothers play a key role in his life as we will see later on in our study. And I am sure you may already know exactly what I am talking about since, like me, you probably grew up in church hearing, drawing, or even acting out the life of Joseph. I would be tickled beyond belief if you sat down to this study having never read the Biblical account of Joseph! If that is the case, you are in for a real treat, my dear! However, whether you already know the narrative or not, I may be safe in assuming you might not be as familiar with what some of Joseph's brothers were really like. Don't worry I wasn't really aware of the extent of their devious natures prior to writing this study! So let's dig into the Word together and investigate what the lives of Joseph's brothers were like prior to their unruly dealings with Joseph.

Just so that we can visually see who's who, I have written the names of Jacob's wives, their maidservants, and their sons (Gen 35:23-26) and want you to circle only Rachel's biological sons.

Leah: Reuben, Simeon, Levi, Judah, Issachar, and Zebulun.

Rachel: Joseph and Benjamin

Bilhah (Rachel's Maidservant): Dan and Naphtali

Zilpah (Leah's Maidservant): Gad and Asher

Jacob had an encounter where he literally wrestled with God and the Lord changed his name to Israel.

The names of these twelve boys, who all share the same father, Jacob, would comprise what we know as the twelve tribes of Israel. Jacob had an encounter where he literally wrestled with God and the Lord changed his name to Israel. "God said to him, 'Your name is Jacob, but you will no longer be called Jacob; your name will be Israel.' So He named him Israel" (Gen 35:10). Hence, the reason we have the twelve tribes of Israel instead of the twelve tribes of Jacob. There are so many wonderful details into the life of Jacob and his father Isaac and grandfather Abraham. You may have at one time already studied these great Patriarchs but if you have not, I strongly encourage you to read the whole book of Genesis, starting with the very first chapter! You don't have to do it today but maybe when you have finished our study. By then, I may have peaked your interest!

If we focus our attention once again on the brothers, we will find some shady behavior among them. The older of the twelve were Reuben, Simeon, Levi, and Judah, all four sharing Leah as their mother. Scripture gives us a very disturbing account of the behavior of some of these older brothers, particularly Simeon and Levi. But before we look at the situation together, let me give you just a little backstory. After living with Rachel and Leah's father, Laban, for twenty years, Jacob was ready to go back to his homeland. He initially fled from the anger of his twin brother Esau after deceptively taking his birthright, which held all the incentives given only to the firstborn son (Gen

27:1-46). Esau had come out of the womb first so he was considered the first one born of the twins (25:19-34). Long story short, Jacob and his mother Rebekah feared that Esau would kill Jacob for taking his birthright and therefore Jacob fled to his uncle's hometown, eventually marrying Rachel and Leah. There he, his wives, and children remained up until he sensed that Laban's attitude toward him began to change (31:2). There was an issue with the livestock acquired by Jacob. Laban began to suspect Jacob was swindling him out of his property, even though Laban had already agreed to give Jacob a certain breed of goats as his wages (30:25-43). Nevertheless, the Lord was the one who showed favor to Jacob and one night through a dream, gave him the wisdom on how to deal with Laban.

In breeding season I once had a dream in which I looked up and saw that the male goats mating with the flock were streaked, speckled, or spotted. The angel of God said to me in a dream, 'Jacob,' I answered, 'Here I am.' And He said, 'Look up and see that all the male goats mating with the flock are streaked, speckled or spotted, for I have seen all that Laban has been doing to you. I am the God of Bethel, where you anointed a pillar and where you made a vow to Me. Now leave this land at once and go back to your native land (Gen 31:10-13).

Even through his uncle's dream, the Lord continued to prove to Jacob that He was the One deemed to be His ultimate protector!

I find it so endearing that God was the one keeping track of how Laban had treated Jacob the twenty years he had been with him, especially His noticing the deception of giving Jacob not just one of his daughters in marriage, but two! We tend to forget that God truly cares about the way we are treated by others and that He takes personal responsibility for us. That is exactly why we can let Him be our true Defender and show us favor without us trying to be vindictive or vengeful to those who have wronged us.

Jesus lives to intercede for us every second of every minute, every minute of every hour, every hour of every day, and every day of every year.

When Jacob, with his wives, children, servants and livestock finally left Laban, they were not very popular! Laban pursued them, potentially with the intent to harm Jacob, but even then, the Lord came to Jacob's defense. Laban said, "I have the power to harm you; but last night the God of your father said to me, 'Be careful not to say anything to Jacob, either good or bad'" (Gen 31:29). Even through his uncle's dream, the Lord continued to prove to Jacob that He was the One deemed to be His ultimate protector!

Do you trust the Lord to truly defend you? Do you believe He has the power and desire to take personal responsibility for you?

Reading accounts of God's workings in His children, like Jacob, reminds me of how wonderful a Savior and Defender is our God! "…for their Defender is strong; He will take up their case…" (Proverbs 23:11). If our Savior took full responsibility for our sin on the Cross, I don't think He would stop there. In fact, I know He doesn't. He sees us all the way through to the end of our lives and everything in between. "Wherefore He is able also to save them to the uttermost that come unto God by Him, seeing He ever liveth to make intercession for them" (Hebrews 7:25, KJV). Jesus lives to intercede for us every second of every minute, every minute of every hour, every hour of every day, and every day of every year. He will see us through it all, from yesterday to today, and for all eternity! We can trust Him!

Jacob was learning to trust God and God continued to prove Himself faithful to Jacob. However, his sons, particularly the eldest ones, seemed to harbor more of a rebellious rather than reverent heart toward God. Now the only way for us to really understand the whole story of what took place with some of the eldest brothers we are going to have to read Genesis 34...yes, the whole thing! Don't worry, once you start reading it, you will be hooked! Then you will have the opportunity to exercise your reading comprehension by answering the couple of questions that follow, similar to the assignments I give my homeschool girls! I bet you didn't think this homeschool momma had it in her to throw some of my day job skills at you…but I do!

Read Genesis 34:1-31 in your Bible.

What were the names of Leah's daughter, her violator, and the violator's father (34:1-2)?

What role did Simeon and Levi play in the incident and how did Jacob respond to their actions (34:25-31)?

Clearly, the older brothers were looking out for their little sister and rightfully so, however, their vengeful act showed a disturbing hostility which brooded within their hearts.

So far we have only highlighted the sons born to Jacob, but here we read an account of his one and only daughter, Dinah, who was born sometime later after Leah's last maternal son, Zebulun.

Leah conceived again and bore Jacob a sixth son. Then Leah said, "God has presented me with a precious gift. This time my husband will treat me with honor, because I borne him six sons." So she named him Zebulun. Sometime later she gave birth to a daughter and named her Dinah (Gen 30:19-21).

Clearly, the older brothers were looking out for their little sister and rightfully so, however, their vengeful act showed a disturbing hostility which brooded within their hearts.

If you have been the victim of a terrible act of violence, I want you to know that my heart aches for you.

When Jacob heard that his daughter Dinah had been defiled, his sons were in the fields with his livestock; so he kept quiet about it until they came home. Then Shechem's father Hamor went out to talk with Jacob. Now Jacob's sons had come in from the fields as soon as they heard what happened. They were filled with grief and fury, because Shechem had done a disgraceful thing in Israel by lying with Jacob's daughter–a thing that should not be done (Gen 34:6-7).

Disgraceful is an understatement! The deception that followed on behalf of the brothers lust for revenge could have resulted not only in their deaths but the deaths of Jacob and the whole entire family. If you have been the victim of a terrible act of violence, I want you to know that my heart aches for you. I know many women who have been taken advantage of by men in their past, myself included. Never stay quiet about such violations, but always tell someone if you have been raped, especially the authorities. Dinah was a victim and the attention should have been for her justice, not for the slaying of so many innocent men. Shechem's desire to marry her may have been genuine. However, Scripture does not even tell us if Dinah wanted to marry him after his actions toward her. Jacob and the brothers could have decided to pack up the family right then and leave town after such a terrible act done to their sister, but instead, the brother's wanted revenge! Revenge is never ours to take. "Do not take revenge, my dear friends, but leave room for God's wrath, for it is written: 'It is Mine to avenge; I will repay,'" says the Lord (Romans 12:19). Jacob had understood this in his dealings with his uncle, Laban, and brother, Esau, but his sons had to learn it themselves. Yet, God's mercy over Jacob and his family saved them from certain death after the slaying of the Shechemite men.

Then God said to Jacob, "Go up to Bethel and settle there, and build an altar there to God, who appeared to you when you were fleeing from your brother. So Jacob said to his household and to all who were with him, "Get rid of the foreign gods you have with you, and purify yourselves and change your clothes. Then come, let us go up to Bethel, where I will build an altar to God, who answered me in the day of my distress and who has been with me wherever I have gone. So they gave Jacob all the foreign gods they had and the rings in their ears, and Jacob buried them under the oak tree at Shechem. Then they set out, and the terror of God fell upon the towns all around them so that no one pursued them (Gen 35:1-5).

Jacob's sons did not get the punishment they deserved for their vengeful actions. Instead, their father called the whole family to a time of cleansing and repentance. Bethel means "House of God," and it was the very place where the Lord had already appeared to Jacob during a glorious dream. So Jacob not only went to this place himself, but took the whole family and called them to worship. "Get rid of the foreign gods you have with you, purify yourselves and change your clothes. Then come up to Bethel..." (35:2-3). Oh, sweet friend, the symbolism here is unfathomable because we have a Heavenly Father who calls us to do the very same thing. He calls us to repentance through the precious blood of Christ Jesus, since He Himself chose *not* to give us what our actions deserved.

Jacob's sons did not get the punishment they deserved for their revengeful actions. Instead, their father called the whole family to a time of cleansing and repentance.

He calls us to repentance since He Himself, through the precious blood of Christ Jesus, chose *not* to give us what our actions deserved.

When you were dead in your sins and in the uncircumcision of your flesh, God made you alive with Christ. He forgave us all our sins, having canceled the charge of our legal indebtedness, which stood against us and condemned us; He has taken it away, nailing it to the cross (Colossians 2:13-14).

If we confess our sins, He is faithful and just and will forgive us our sins and purify us from all unrighteousness (1 John 1:9).

Similar to Jacob's family, we must enter the House of God (that place in our hearts where Christ desires to dwell with us) and continually confess our sin in order to experience a cleansing from all the defilement of the world. Do you struggle with selfishness, anger, bitterness, resentment, addiction, unbelief, anxiety or whatever else threatens to keep you from experiencing freedom in Christ? Maybe you need to imagine yourself taking the trip with Jacob's family, changing the attitude of your mind, and purifying your heart from worldly infiltration. Genuine repentance is a deliberate act of the will and will always yield a visible change seen in the way we daily live our lives, emphasis on *daily*!

If you were with Jacob's family, what specifically would you lay on the altar at Bethel?

If you have never confessed your sin before God and asked Christ into your heart in order to receive His salvation and forgiveness of sin, then I pray that is something you will consider doing right now!

If you have never confessed your sin before God and asked Christ into your heart in order to receive His salvation and forgiveness of sin, then I pray that is something you will consider doing right now! If you want to pray this simple prayer with me, in faith, do so now.

Pray, "Lord, forgive me of my sin, I desire for you to come into my life and change me. I know that following You not only means praying this prayer, but also seeking to live a life of obedience to You and following Your commands written in the Bible. I confess that You are Lord and by faith acknowledge that if I place my trust in You, You will save me from an eternity in hell. Thank you, Lord, for Your salvation! In Jesus name, Amen."

If you prayed that prayer, then I want you to find your Bible study teacher or leader in your church and tell them the decision that you have made to follow Christ and make His the Lord of your life! I know today's homework was long so thank you for hanging in there and I promise tomorrow with be shorter! You are such a blessing to me!

Day Four: Deep Sorrow, Deceptive Seduction

Often we mistakenly idolize the characters of Scripture and think that because they had visions, dreamed dreams, heard the very voice of God speaking clearly or even visibly saw angels, that is was easier for them to be full of faith.

So far we have seen a side of Joseph's older brothers which has been less than becoming. Sadly, their time of repentance and worship at Bethel was short lived, reminding us that Jacob's life as a father and husband was full of hardship. Often we mistakenly idolize the characters of Scripture and think that because they had visions, dreamed dreams, heard the very voice of God speaking clearly or even visibly saw angelic beings, that it was easier for them to be full of faith. The truth is they had it rough. Even just the era in which they lived was itself much different and far more difficult than ours today. No cars, airplanes, hospitals, subdivisions, you name it and chances are, they didn't have it! To this day, in the desert region, where the patriarchs of the Bible traveled, it is still very barren and not equipped with the resources we have in our part of the world. Sometimes we just need to stop and thank the Lord for the comforts He has given us, even when we experience some less than comfortable seasons. Chances are we still have so much more than most!

What are you thankful for today, right this moment? Lift up a prayer of thanksgiving before we dig into today's lesson.

Let's be honest, you may be in an extremely trying season right now and find it hard to be thankful for anything.

Let's be honest, you may be in an extremely trying season right now and find it hard to be thankful for anything. I get that, I really do and if this is where you are then you will be able to relate to Jacob's state of mind today as we study a season of great loss for him, which was followed by bitter disgust. And sadly, we will read of more loss to come for poor Jacob as we continue throughout our study. Hardship is a way of life and has been since the fall of man. Yet it's the anguishing adversities that reveal the ache in our souls for the full redemption of all mankind. Rest assured, full redemption will come one day, when Christ returns and seals the fate of sin and death, creating a new heaven and earth where righteousness will reign forever and His kingdom shall never come to an end! Nevertheless, until that day comes, our faith will continue to grow in ways that we simply cannot comprehend this side of Heaven through the very trials placed along the path we call life. One of the most challenging difficulties we all are confronted with is losing those we love so deeply. Jacob was no exception to experiencing such tragedy himself.

What happened after Jacob and his family moved on from Bethel (Genesis 35:16-20)?

After staying some time in Bethel, Jacob moved on. Rachel, pregnant with her second biological son, began to feel the birth pains of labor. Yet, unlike the birth of Joseph, Rachel had great difficulty with the birth of Benjamin.

And as she was having great difficulty in childbirth, the midwife said to her, "Don't be afraid, for you have another son." As she breathed her last–for she was dying–she named her son Ben-Oni [son of my trouble][8]. But his father named him Benjamin [son of my right hand][9] (Gen 35:17-18, brackets mine).

Rachel's death just breaks my heart. You know Jacob could not wait to get his entire family back to his father, Isaac, and introduce his prized wife! To show off the woman he loved the most from the very beginning, the woman he waited seven years, one month, and one week to marry, then another seven years after that! Whether or not Jacob should have opened his heart to Leah, we cannot fault him for being truly in love with one woman and wanting nothing more than to present her to his beloved mother and father.

[8] *NIV Comparative Study Bible*, footnote "Ben-Oni," pg 97. Zondervan, Grand Rapids, MI: 1999.
[9] Ibid, "Benjamin."

As I was returning from Paddan (that is, Northwest Mesopotamia), to my sorrow Rachel died in the land of Canaan while we were still on the way, a little distance from Ephrath. So I buried her there beside the road to Ephrath (that is, Bethlehem) (Gen 48:7).

Have you ever felt as though circumstances brought life to a complete halt while you or those you loved "were still on the way" to making plans, fulfilling desires, or dreaming dreams of a bright future?

We do not know the number of our days on this earth. Some of us may have many while others may have very few. "A person's days are determined; You have decreed the number of his months and have set limits he cannot exceed" (Job 14:5). God's original plan was for us to live for eternity and for Adam and Eve to never even taste death. However, once sin entered the world through the temptation of Adam and Eve eating from the tree of the knowledge of good and evil, death became the cruel fate for mankind. Yet, through Jesus Christ, death no longer leads to an eternal dead end! Praise the Lord! I have no idea why some people live only a few weeks in the womb, while others live to be one hundred years old. Maybe you didn't lose someone, yet there were other circumstances which brought your plans or dreams for the future to a complete halt. No matter the case, we can trust our God whose wisdom and mercy knows no bounds and who has plans that far exceed the visible, earthly realm of our immediate reality. So all I can say is hold on to your Savior and Mighty Deliverer and wait for Him to do what only He can do with your remaining days on this earth.

Yet, through Jesus Christ, death no longer leads to an eternal deal end!

So all I can say is hold on to your Savior and Mighty Deliverer and wait for Him to do what only He can do with your remaining days on this earth.

Jacob's remaining days after the loss of Rachel still held within them immense challenges, one of those challenges being not long after the burial of his beloved wife.

Israel moved on again and pitched his tent beyond Migdal Eder. While Israel was living in that region, Reuben went in and slept with his father's concubine, Bilhah, and Israel heard of it (Gen 35:21-22).

Not many miles away from Bethlehem, where Jacob buried Rachel, and still on their way to Jacob's hometown, the family set up camp again in Migdal Eder. While there, Reuben committed a grievous sin against his father. It seems, since there is no mention of how Jacob felt, that he may not have been angry about it. By the way, I am still calling Jacob, Jacob, in order for us not to get confused. However, his name at this point in Scripture is also referred to as Israel. Regardless of there being mention of it or not, Jacob was deeply troubled that Reuben slept with Bilhah. Additionally, Jacob was still grieving the loss of his wife when his firstborn son carelessly and heartlessly went behind his back and committed adultery with his concubine.

If you have children, has there ever been a time when they wounded you so deeply, doing almost the unthinkable during a time of crisis for your family?

You may or may not have experienced anything as Jacob did with his son Rueben, but I am sure you have felt betrayal in some form from your children, husband or other family members. Jacob certainly felt betrayed and we see later on in Scripture where the consequences of Reuben's sin finally caught up with him.

What did Jacob prophecy over Reuben on his deathbed, at the end of his life (Gen 49:1-4)?

The *Amplified Bible* translates *Genesis 49:3-4* in a way which gives us more insight into how Jacob may have really felt about Reuben's actions.

Reuben, you are my firstborn, my might, the beginning (the firstfruits) of my manly strength and vigor; [your birthright gave you] the preeminence in dignity and the preeminence in power. But unstable and boiling over like water, you shall not excel and have the preeminence [of the firstborn], because you went to your father's bed; you defiled it–he went to my couch! [Gen. 35:22]

Maybe you know individuals who push the limits and test God by habitual sinning with an unrepentant heart and it seems like God is silent on the matter.

Reuben may have thought his father had forgotten about what he did some years ago with Bilhah by the time Jacob gave the final blessings to his sons. However, the long awaited consequences most certainly caught up with him and instead of receiving the inheritance of the first born, it was given to Joseph. Does it ever seem as though sin is left unchecked by God? Maybe you know individuals who push the limits and test God by habitual sinning with an unrepentant heart and it seems like God is silent on the matter. The apostle Paul addresses this issue very pointedly in Romans when speaking of those who go about sinning with an unrepentant heart.

But because of your stubbornness and your unrepentant heart, you are storing up wrath against yourself for the day of God's wrath, when His righteous judgment will be revealed. God will give to each person according to what he has done. To those who by persistence in doing good seek glory, honor and immortality, He will give eternal life. But for those who are self-seeking and who reject truth and follow evil, there will be wrath and anger... This will take place on the day when God will judge men's secrets through Jesus Christ, as my gospel declares (Romans 2:5-8, 16).

The phrase, "storing up wrath against yourself," is a scary thought! I am so very grateful that God's promises to forgive our sins and "cleanse us from all unrighteousness" if we confess our sins to Him (1 John 1:9). If we harbor a repentant spirit and continually confess our sin to the Lord, He will forgive us and remember our sin no more. Therefore, "on the day when God will judge men's secrets though Jesus Christ," we will have no secret sins since we already confessed them to the Lord and received His forgiveness (Rom 2:8).

Have you ever worried about judgment day and what sins might be brought against you from your past?

I used to be so worried that when I died, there would be a giant movie screen that the Lord and I would have to watch together so that I could give an account for everything I had ever done, good and bad. But when I began to really study God's Word, I realized that I would only have to give an account for the things I did with a stubborn and unrepentant heart, having never sought forgiveness. So you better believe that I do a lot of confessing of my sin on a daily basis in order not to have to give an account for being prideful in my sin! Another consolation in this same vein of thought is found in *Psalm 103:10-14*.

...He does not treat us as our sins deserve or repay us according to our iniquities. For as high as the heavens are above the earth, so great is His love for those who fear Him; as far as the east is from the west, so far has He removed our transgressions from us. As a father has compassion on his children so the Lord has compassion on those who fear Him; for He knows how we are formed, He remembers that we are dust.

If those verses don't give you hope, sister, I don't know what will! Think about this...if God has removed our transgressions from us, as far as the east is from the west, do you think He is doing to go drag up those sins and make us give an account for something He Himself has chosen to forget? I don't think so. Oh, my friend, we are loved so much more than we deserve by our Lord and Savior Jesus Christ. The Cross *fully* paid the price for *all* our sin! We just need to be faithful to stay humble and be willing to continually confess our sins before the Lord so He can remove them far from us. So on that note, I want you to rejoice the rest of this day, knowing that you are loved and forgiven!

I want you to rejoice the rest of this day, knowing you are loved and forgiven!

Day Five: New Favorite

I hope by the end of our first week of study, we begin to understand, to some degree, the kind of shape Jacob (Israel) is in emotionally, as we start to highlight the life of his son, Joseph. Although, before we meet our strapping young teenager, there is one more goodbye Jacob must say to a very important man in his life.

How did Jacob's father, Isaac, feel about Jacob (Genesis 25:28)?

Choosing favorites seemed to run in the family. Even Isaac's father and mother, Abraham and Sarah, favored him more than his brother Ishmael, the son born of Sarah's maidservant, Hagar (Gen 21:8-12). Then Isaac ended up loving Esau more than Jacob or at least showing him more attention simply because Isaac and Esau both had a "taste for wild game," possibly meaning that they enjoyed hunting and gaming together (25:28). I think we tend to do this in our own families by saying of a son, "he's definitely a momma's boy," or of a daughter, she is "daddy's girl." I even say this of my own daughters since they love their daddy so much. However, just because Kate (my oldest) gravitates more to her father when all four of us are together, it doesn't mean that he loves her more than Lily Beth (my youngest). If a parent makes it clear that they love one sibling more than the other, that show of favoritism can be extremely damaging to the other children in the family. Honestly, it is hard to say how Isaac really felt about Jacob, but I tend to think he still loved him as a father loves a son, even if he did have more in common with his oldest son, Esau. Nevertheless, most of Jacob's adult life was spent away from his father and mother, while living under his uncle, Laban. When Jacob finally arrived home after their long journey, I hope they were able to rekindle their relationship up to the last days of Isaac's life (but we really don't know since we are not given any more details in Scripture).

I know there are some parents who make it clear that they love one sibling more than the other. That show of favoritism can be extremely damaging to the other children in the family.

Jacob came home to his father Isaac in Mamre, near Kiriath Arba (that is, Hebron), where Abraham and Isaac had stayed. Isaac lived a hundred and eighty years. Then he breathed his last and died and was gathered to his people, old and full of years. And his sons Esau and Jacob buried him (Gen 35:27-29).

So if we recap the events of Jacob's life up to this point, here's what we've got:

-He felt as though his father favored his brother over him (Gen 25:28).

-He deceitfully, under the encouragement of his mother, stole his brother's blessing (Gen 27).

-He ran for his life to his uncle Laban's house and was tricked by his uncle into marrying Rachel's sister Leah (Gen 29).

-He dealt with his constantly quarreling wives over who would have more children (Gen 29:31-30:24).

-He was misunderstood by Laban, fled from him, then nearly had a stroke thinking his brother Esau would kill him and his whole family when he saw him again. (Gen 31-32).

-He wrestled with God during all of his running from Laban and Esau and was literally crippled for life by the encounter (Gen 33:22-32).

-He feared for his life and family's lives after his daughter was raped by Shechem and then his sons decided to murder all of the men in the city (Gen 34)!

-His wife, Rachel, died during childbirth before he reached his father's home (Gen 35:16-19).

-His oldest son slept with Leah's maidservant, Bilhah (Gen 35:22).

-His father, Isaac, died (Gen 35:28-29).

Now you may be wondering why I was so intent on giving such an overview of Jacob's life. Clearly, we only briefly touched on a few of the hardships he faced but what I am really trying to help us understand is that there may have been a reason for how he felt about his son Joseph.

All my life I had pegged Jacob as this mean father who cared nothing for his other sons based on this one verse.

Now Israel loved Joseph more than any of his other sons, because he had been born to him in his old age... (Gen 37:3a).

Do you think having Joseph in his old age made Jacob love him more?

Do you see why I wanted us to really get a sense of all Jacob had been through prior to us reading this one verse about how, "Israel loved Joseph more than any of his other sons...?" All my life I had pegged Jacob as this mean father who cared nothing for his other sons based on this one verse. I never stopped to investigate what the older sons were like and how much Jacob's love for Rachel fueled his love for the firstborn of her womb. Remember, Rachel herself only bore Jacob two sons, Joseph and Benjamin. And also remember that Jacob never asked or intended to marry Leah, but was tricked by his uncle Laban. Now, I am not giving Jacob permission not to love his other sons. However, after studying his life and the life of his sons more in depth, I can understand why Jacob, in his old age, having lived an extremely difficult life, would have showed more favoritism to Joseph.

These next couple of questions are merely meant for me to relay a point, so if they do not apply to you, don't worry. Just answer the best you can.

Do you have a much younger sibling, let's say ten to fifteen years younger?

Do your parents, mother or father, depending on if there is a step parent involved, give things to that much younger sibling that they never gave you when you were that age?

Now do you get insanely jealous when your much younger sibling is seemly treated more favorable because they are so young and still under the roof of your parent or parents?

If you said yes to all three, we may have to have a talk about that last question! But chances are you understand, mainly because of your age and maturity, that the younger siblings, especially much younger siblings, would be kept near their father and let's say, spoiled a bit. When Joseph and Benjamin were born, it would have been similar to Jacob having grandsons. Now we all know how much differently grandparents treat our children! Like letting them eat way too much sugar before sending them back home to us and buying them all sorts of unnecessary items simply because they want to spoil them rotten! This is just the general rule of grandparents, or at least some grandparents. We do not live close to any of the girl's grandparents but still get gifts in the mail and the occasional spoiling during visits. So even if your situation is very different, I am sure you are getting the picture of Joseph's family dynamic. He and Benjamin are the babies of the family. Not only that, they were young boys who had experienced great loss right along with their father. Benjamin never knew his mother, since she died giving birth to him. And Joseph was very young, only a small boy, when his mother passed away. Both boys, quite possibly in their teenage years or a little younger, experienced the loss of their grandfather, Isaac. I can only imagine that they would have clung to their father and their father to them. Plus, their track record, compared to their older brothers was clean. They hadn't yet lived long enough to make some of the choices as their eldest siblings had.

So even if your situation is very different, I am sure you are getting the picture of Joseph's family dynamic.

How does getting the whole picture, or at least our best attempt, help you to understand Joseph's position in the family at the age of seventeen?

I don't know if you can tell, but I like to step back and try to see a story from as many angles as possible! We were not there, so we have to speculate so many things. Yet, after putting some pieces together, hopefully we have a clearer understanding of where we meet Joseph and how so much of his life up to this point was impacted by his family dynamic. Next week we will continue to see even more intrigue and will have to brace ourselves in order to study Joseph's painful reality for the next decade of his life. Thank you for a great first week of study! I have thoroughly enjoyed it and I hope you have too!

Next week we will continue to see more intrigue and will have to brace ourselves in order to study Joseph's painful reality for the next decade of his life.

LESSON ONE

The Sanctified Socket

Until then he [Jacob] had been a saved man; afterward he became a spiritual man. –Phillips[10]

I. Left alone and having released all he possessed, Jacob was finally ready to ______________ & _____________ with a past he'd always run away from (Genesis 32:22-24).

II. "…a Man wrestled with him till daybreak" (Gen 32:24).

–The "____________ of the Lord" is a distinct person in Himself from God the Father. He must of necessity be One of the "three–in–one Godhead. He does not appear as the "Angel of the Lord" again after Christ came in human form.[11]

–"God meets us at whatever ______________ He finds us in order to __________us to where He wants us to be."[12]

III. God will weaken our dependency on the _______________ while strengthening our dependency on Him through _______________ (Gen 32:25).

–Our _____________________ are a reminder of His ____________________.

IV. Have we ______________ onto God's promises long enough to see them _______________ in our lives (Gen 32:26)?

V. Jacob, "supplanter, schemer, trickster, swindler"[13] (Gen 32:27)

–2 Corinthians 5:17

–Israel, "contender with God," "struggles with God" (Gen 32:28)[14]

VI. In the times of his most devastating _______________, Jacob's _____________ served as a reminder of his dependency on the Lord to help him persevere under great trial (Gen 32:30-32).

---

[10] Phillips, John. *Exploring People of the Old Testament*. pg. 147. Kregal Publications, Grand Rapids, MI: 2006.
[11] *NIV Comparative Study Bible*, footnote. "The Angel of the Lord". pg 38. Zondervan, Grand Rapids, MI: 1999.
[12] Wiersbe, Warren. *The Wiersbe Bible Commentary*. pg. 110. David C. Cook, Colorado Springs, CO., 2007.
[13] *NIV Comparative Study Bible*. Amplified Bible Version. (Gen 32:27). pg 90. Zondervan, Grand Rapids, MI: 1999.
[14] Ibid, (Gen 32:28).

GROUP DISCUSSION QUESTIONS:
The Sanctified Socket

1. Drawing from this past week's homework, what were some of the difficulties Joseph's father, Jacob, had already faced in his life?

2. Can you remember a time in your life where you also "wrestled" or "got dusty" with God and the experience changed you?

3. The Lord changed Jacob's name to Israel to show a change in his character. Try to think of some descriptive words to describe what you were like before you came to Christ, contrasted then with what you are like now that you are in Christ.

4. Jacob was left with a physical weakness as a reminder of his spiritual strength and dependency on the Lord. Are you dealing with a weakness that could serve as a reminder of the Lord's strength working in your life?

WEEK TWO:
Forsaken Though Not Forgotten

Day One: Harassed and Hated

A young man of seventeen, Joseph had lived a life which no doubt made him wise beyond his years.

At the end of last week, we finally met Joseph! We saw how he had grown up as a boy among men since most of his brothers were much older than he. Not to mention that so much of his young life was also lived in transition, moving from place to place, and experiencing the terror among the family when chased after by his grandfather Laban and uncle, Esau. We also were made aware of how he had lost his mother at a very young age, as well as his beloved grandfather, Isaac. A young man of seventeen, Joseph had lived a life which no doubt made him wise beyond his years. And not only did Jacob have a great affection for his firstborn of Rachel, but also an abounding hope that he would continue to prove to be a son who acted obediently in the eyes of his father.

Whom do you think Jacob would give more responsibility in the family business of shepherding, Joseph or his often rebellious older sons?

Seems to me that once Joseph was old enough to be given household responsibilities, he took them with little to no complaints. He was probably eager to please his father and work alongside his older brothers.

Joseph, a young man of seventeen, was tending the flocks with his brothers, the sons of Bilhah and the sons of Zilpah, his father's wives... (Gen 37:2a)

It's amazing to me how many great men of the Bible, especially the Old Testament, were first shepherds before they were chosen of God for special, prophetic, and even kingly tasks.

Look back at Gen 35:25-26 and write down the names of Bilhah and Zilpah's sons.

Later we will read that Joseph was with all the brothers at one point, but when we first encounter his whereabouts, we read here that he tended the flocks with only four of his brothers, Dan, Naphtali, Gad, and Asher. So now we know that one of Joseph's responsibilities was his being a shepherd of his father's flocks. It's amazing to me how many great men of the Bible, especially the Old Testament, were first shepherds before they were chosen of God for special, prophetic, and even kingly tasks. I'm sure one example of this that came to your mind was King David. Remember he was a shepherd long before he became king of Israel. So Joseph was no exception to needing the experience of shepherding animals before being given the opportunity to shepherd people as we will see later on in our study.

What do you think are some of the character virtues that can be obtained from having the occupation of a shepherd?

Joseph came from a long line of shepherds including his father, grandfather, great grandfather and even his mother, Rachel, who was a shepherdess (Gen 29:9). Shepherds and shepherdesses took great care tending the animals. The *Wycliffe Bible Dictionary* gives us some insight to the specific tasks of a sheepherder.

> It was the duty of the sheepherder to lead his flock to pasture and fresh water (Psalm 23:3). In some instances this necessitated long treks across the countryside. In Bible lands it was the custom for the shepherd to lead his sheep rather than to drive them (John 10:4). Another necessary task was that of protecting the flock from wild animals (1 Sam 17:34-35) and robbers (John 10:1). At night the shepherd led his sheep to a place of shelter and protection, such as a fold or natural enclosure (see Sheepcote), where he counted them to see that none had strayed (Jeremiah 33:13; cf. Luke 15:3-7). At lambing time the shepherd gave special care to the ewes and the lambs (Isa 40:11).[15]

You may not be leading sheep but chances are you are leading someone.

What are some of the responsibilities God has placed on you that may resemble the tasks of a shepherd?

You may not be leading sheep but chances are you are leading someone. It may be your children, your aging parents, your aging husband, a class of young students, employees, or a group of young women in a Bible study. Whomever or wherever it may be, you are most likely tending to the needs, whether spiritual or physical, of those who need your tender care. One of the main roles of the shepherd was to meet the basic needs of the sheep by leading them to pasture and fresh water. Yet another role just as equally important was for the shepherd to protect the sheep from wild animals and robbers. A sheepcote or sheepfold was the enclosure used to enclose the sheep at night in order for them to sleep safely. This was similar to a sheep pen except they were generally made out of stone since wood was not a common resource in the desert regions of Israel. And because they were made of stone, usually there was not a door to close the sheep in, but rather the shepherd would sleep in the door way by himself, being the gate for the sheep.[16]

How does Jesus beautifully describe Himself using this analogy of the sheep and the sheepfold in John 10:1-11?

I am the Good Shepherd; I know My sheep and my sheep know Me...John 10:14

I absolutely love how Jesus is our Chief Shepherd, watching over us, protecting us, surrounding us with His presence, and being the One who gives us the freedom to graze under His watchful eye. Jesus also made an interesting statement about those who are hired to watch the sheep.

The hired hand is not the shepherd who owns the sheep. So when he sees the wolf coming, he abandons the sheep and runs away. Then the wolf attacks the flock and it scatters. The man runs away because he is hired and cares nothing for the sheep. I am the Good Shepherd; I know My sheep and my sheep know Me– just as the Father knows Me and I know the Father–and I lay down My life for the sheep (John 10:12-15).

---

[15] Pfeiffer, Charles F., Vos, Howard F., Rea, John, *Wycliffe Bible Dictionary.* Pg. 1238, "Shepherd." Hendrickson Publishers, Inc: Mass, 2001.
[16] Ibid, pg. 1569, "Sheepcote, Sheepfold."

While we must admire Joseph's courage, we can understand how he would not be very popular with the boys of Bil and Zil!

Though we do not know exactly how Jacob's older sons, Dan, Naphtali, Gad, and Asher, were treating the sheep, we do know that after Joseph had been tending the flocks with them, "he brought back a bad report about them" (Gen 37:2b). The sons, of course, were not hired hands since they were Jacob's sons, but it is likely they could have acted like it to some degree. Theologian, F.B. Meyer says, "Joseph was endowed with very remarkable intelligence. It would almost seem as if he were chief shepherd (v.2), the sons of Bilhah and Zilpah acting as his subordinates and assistants."[17] As we read in Gen 37:3, Jacob, having had Joseph in his old age, loved him more than his other sons, but one reason for that may have been that Jacob saw a unique leadership quality in Joseph. Therefore, he appointed him as overseer of his brothers while they were grazing the flocks. No doubt this probably severely irritated his much older brothers with them having to take orders from their younger, favored, seventeen year old brother! In loyalty to his father and at the risk of making trouble with his brothers, Jospeh tells Jacob the truth about their behavior by bringing back a bad report. While we must admire Joseph's courage, we can understand how he would not be very popular with the boys of Bil and Zil! Then to add injury to insult, Jacob doesn't do Joseph any favors in the area of brotherly love with the next show of favoritism. "...and he (Jacob) made a richly ornamented robe for him" (Gen 37:3b, *parentheses mine*).

When his brothers saw that their father loved him more than any of them, they hated him and could not speak a kind word to him (Gen 37:4).

But the coat, the famous robe, caught the attention of the brothers and even the secular world today, forever pairing Joseph with such a coat of many colors.

Well, no wonder! Joseph, the younger brother, is placed as overseer of his much older brothers, then he delivers a bad report about them, and to top it all off, their father makes him a robe! I didn't know Jacob could sew, did you? He sure could and he sure did! I can imagine there were many more shows of favoritism up to where we meet Joseph in chapter 37. But the coat, the famous robe, caught the attention of the brothers and even the secular world today, forever pairing Joseph with such a glamorous coat of many colors.

If you grew up hearing the story of Joseph, what image comes to mind when thinking of his coat of many colors?

Even if you didn't grow up hearing the story and seeing the pictures, even coloring the pictures of Joseph's colorful coat, you might imagine a stripped, multi-colored tunic or outer robe. F. B. Meyer once again gives us another thought to ponder or image to bring to mind that may be a little closer to the reality of what Joseph's famous garment looked like and why the brothers were so angry at the sight of it!

> We may have been accustomed to think of this coat as a kind of patchwork quilt, and we have wondered that grown men should have been moved to such passion at the sight of the peacock plumes of their younger brother. But further knowledge will correct these thoughts. The Hebrew word means simply a tunic reaching to the extremities, and describes a garment commonly worn in Egypt and the adjacent lands. Imagine a long white linen robe extending to the ankles and wrists, and embroidered with a narrow stripe of color round the edge of the skirt and sleeves, and you will have a very fair conception of this famous coat. *Now we can understand the envy of his brothers. This sort of robe was worn only by the opulent and noble, by kings' sons, and by those who had no need to toil for their living. All who had to win their bread by labor wore short, colored garments that did not show stain or cramp the free movement of*

[17] Meyer, F.B. *Joseph, Beloved, Hated, Exalted.* pg. 11, CLC Publications: Fort Washington, PA, 2013, Kindle Version.

limbs. Such was the lot of Jacob's sons, and such the garments they wore (Italics mine).[18]

That description makes so much more sense! Instead of the color or ornamentation of the garment or even the fact that Jacob made it for Joseph, the brothers were more enraged at what the tunic represented. How prophetic that it was a robe only worn by kings and nobles in Egypt or the adjacent lands! Joseph had already been placed as the chief shepherd and overseer of his brothers when they tended the flocks and now he wore a coat that not only reminded the brothers of his position but also anyone else who saw them working together.

Instead of the color or ornamentation of the garment or even the fact that Jacob made it for Joseph, the brothers were more enraged at what the tunic represented.

How does Meyer note the significance of the lengths of the garments that Joseph and his brothers wore at the end of his quote?

The length of Joseph's coat automatically placed him in a position where he could not do the same manual labor as his brothers. Their coats were short in case they needed to wade through swamps, clamber up hills, carry wandering sheep home on their shoulders, fight with robbers and beasts of prey; and for such toils a flowing linen robe would have been unfit.[19]

When they saw that their father loved him more than any of them, they hated him and could not speak a kind word to him (Gen 37:4).

Jealously can lead to uncontrollable anger and cause people to do terrible, hateful things. Notice that the bothers hated him so much, they couldn't even speak a kind word to him.

Jealously can lead to uncontrollable anger and cause people to do terrible, hateful things.

Have you ever let jealousy, bitterness, or hate cause you to avoid another person to the extent of not even speaking to them at all when you see them?

We have to be so careful of our heart condition toward other people. We may not realize we are treating them wrongly, but our actions may be speaking louder by our lack of words. If you are convicted at all in this area, confess it to the Lord. He is faithful and He can restore our hearts and how we feel toward others. We have so much ground to cover this week so don't lose momentum, the plot only thickens in the life of Joseph and his brothers. I pray the Lord will astound us with the study of His Word! Thank you for your perseverance today, sister!

Day Two: Dying to a Dream

My heart truly breaks for Joseph. Here we have an innocent young man of seventeen seeking to please the heart of his father and be obedient to his position given as overseer of his older brothers. It makes me wonder if he ever asked his father, why me? He may have said, "But I am the second to youngest, why do you want me to look after my brothers?" And Jacob may have responded by saying, "Son, your older brothers are not pure in heart and do not have in mind the things of God, therefore they cannot be trusted and I need you to look after them, reporting back to me of their behavior." Then for Joseph to be given a beautifully ornamented robe that his father made for him, how could he have refused such a special gift? I fear that for so long we have misunderstood the

[18] Ibid
[19] Ibid

character of our young Joseph. We may have felt that he was spoiled and big headed and provoked his brothers to the point of them hating him. And maybe we didn't think he deserved what all they did to him, but we at least could see why they did it. The thing is this is not only a child's story, merely gleaned for the pages of a children's Bible. This is a true story of a man who was mocked and hated for having a pure heart. This is a young man whose brothers seethed with jealousy and despised him so much that they could not even speak to him without breathing out hate. And that only got worse with time.

This is a true story of a man who was mocked and hated for having a pure heart.

Joseph had a dream, and when he told it to his brothers, they hated him all the more (Gen 37:5).

Joseph, in his youth, may not have even realized how much his brothers really hated him. Maybe he thought they were jealous at times, but not enough to stop him from treating them like family and at times even confiding in them. It is likely that until he was a bit older, Joseph's brothers probably were okay with him or at least more tolerant of him more than they were now. Not to mention that when Rachel was alive, they dared not laid a hand on him. However, Joseph had not yet learned, at the age of seventeen, how to guard his heart and hold his tongue.

Have you ever confided in someone, telling them things that God has placed on your heart, maybe even dreams, only to have them look at you like you are crazy?

There are some things that God reveals to us that we are to keep hidden in our hearts. I have learned this the hard way. I have confided in individuals with the hope that they would be supportive and encouraging only to have them be the very opposite. You may have someone in your life that supports you in whatever dreams, callings, or revelations the Lord lays on your heart. I use the word "dream" loosely here because what we may consider a dream is really a strong desire we feel we have been given by the Lord which He has validated through Scripture and other influences in our lives. However, Joseph had a literal dream; one where he closed his eyes and vividly saw a series of images which required an interpretation. Scholars say it is debatable whether or not the Lord communicates directly or indirectly by dreams in this day, although it is not thought to be impossible.[20] Nevertheless, whatever the way God should choose to reveal something to us, He is still the only one who is able carry it out in our lives. Revelation without destination is no revelation at all. When we are trusted by God with something inspiring, we must wait on Him and His timing. So often we take a dream and run with it, not being sure where we are going! To know if a dream or revelation is truly of God, we must be willing to patiently wait on Him to bring it about. He will always be faithful to show us the steps to take. And quite often, the process is a slow one.

Nevertheless, whatever the way God should choose to reveal something to us, He is still the only one who is able carry it out in our lives.

Has God ever given you a vision and you patiently waited on Him to bring it about?

I have some dear friends who adopted a sweet little girl from China. God moved in their hearts, gave them a vision for adoption, and then they waited for His leading every step of the way. Visions, dreams, moves of God upon our hearts are all wonderful ways that

---

[20] Pfeiffer, Charles F., Vos, Howard F., Rea, John, *Wycliffe Bible Dictionary*. Pg. 475, "Dream." Hendrickson Publishers, Inc: Mass, 2001.

He leads us. However, there are times when the vision is so grand that it sounds absurd to even speak of it to anyone else. This was the case with Joseph.

How did his brothers respond to Joseph's dreams (Gen 37:5 & 8)?

Before we are even told what the dream was, Scripture clearly points out the fact that this dream was the tip of the iceberg! As if his brothers needed any more reason to absolutely despise Joseph!

What do you think Joseph's dreams represented according to the dreams themselves and the reaction of the brothers (Gen 37:6-10)?

As if his brothers needed any more reason to absolutely despise Joseph!

I don't want us to miss the reaction of Jacob to Joseph's dreams either! How did he respond in Gen 37:10?

Here we have two dreams of Joseph. However, the first one seemed to only include the brothers.

We were binding sheaves of grain out in the field when suddenly my sheaf rose and stood upright, while your sheaves gathered around mine and bowed down to it (Gen 37:7).

A sheaf is a stalk "of grain gathered together and tied into a bundle after harvesting."[21] The brothers must have understood very quickly that the stalks represented each of them and Joseph's stalk rising above theirs meant he was going to rule over them. However, what the brothers, or even Joseph for that matter, could not foresee was the prophetic message behind the stalks of wheat. As we will read later on in our study, it would be those very stalks of wheat that Joseph's family would come to seek from him in Egypt. Nevertheless, none of that mattered in the heat of the moment as Joseph was describing his first dream! The Amplified Bible gives us another insight to what they were thinking in its translation of their reaction in verse 8.

However, what the brothers, or even Joseph for that matter, could not foresee was the prophetic message behind the stalks of wheat.

His brothers said to him, Shall you indeed reign over us? Or are you going to have us as your subjects and dominate us? (Gen 37:8a, Amp)

It seems to me that even though Joseph had been made the chief shepherd of the brothers and even though he wore a coat that signified him as such, the brother's still did not take his position seriously. They may have not listened to him at all, but rather rolled their eyes every time Joseph spoke a word of instruction to them. And now that the dream had been made known, they were astonished to think that Joseph may have actually thought he had some sort of authority over them! "Shall you indeed reign over us?" You can almost imagine the perplexity and shock over the absurdity of Joseph's dream written all over their faces.

[21] Lockyer, Herbert. *Nelson's Illustrated Bible Dictionary*. Pg. 973, "sheaf." Thomas Nelson Publishers: Nashville, TN., 1986.

We cannot be certain how much time had passed from Joseph's first dream to the next but if anything, it certainly wasn't enough time for his brothers to have recovered from the shock and horror of the first one!

Then he had another dream, and he told it to his brothers. "Listen, he said, "I had another dream, and this time the sun and moon and eleven stars were bowing down to me" (Gen 37:9).

At this point I think you and I both want to say, "No, Joseph! Don't say anything else to rock the boat with your brothers!"

At this point I think you and I both want to say, "No, Joseph! Don't say anything else to rock the boat with your brothers!" Nevertheless, here goes round two. But this time the dream not only involves the brothers but also mom and dad as well. Remember at this point, Rachel, Joseph's biological mother had passed away. Although, since Leah was still alive, it's most likely that Jacob was referring to her in his reaction to Joseph's dream. "Will your mother and I and your brothers actually come and bow down to the ground before you?" (Gen 37:10b). The sun and moon likely referred to Jacob and Leah and the eleven stars referred to the brothers. The family depicted in the dream by astronomical figures also prophetically represented Joseph's future in Egypt, just as the first dream. The Egyptians worshipped many foreign gods. Some of those gods included animal and human figures as well as cosmic ones.

The Egyptians worshiped the sun, moon, and stars. Ra (also Re), the sun god, was the supreme deity of the ancient Egyptians. When Ra is absent, Throth, the moon, is prominent. But the moon is definitely inferior to the sun.[22] Joseph's dream implied that Jacob (represented by the sun), Leah (the moon) and the brothers (the stars) would all bow down to him one day. No one liked this idea, not even Jacob! Yet, even though Jacob was unsettled by the dream, he still pondered it and Scripture tells us that he, Jacob, "kept the matter in mind" (Gen 37:11b).

Has your child or maybe someone younger, slightly less mature by experience, ever told you a dream they had or a strong desire for what they wanted to be or do when they grew up? If so, how did you respond to that child or individual? What were your thoughts on the issue?

I think his initial reaction was defensive, but then he probably lifted his eyebrows and thought, "Hmm, I wonder what that dream really means for Joseph?"

Chances are that you smiled and pondered the idea of maybe it coming true. My motive in asking you this is really to help us understand what Jacob was thinking in response to Joseph. I think his initial reaction was defensive, but then he probably lifted his eyebrows and thought, "Hmm, I wonder what that dream really means for Joseph?" Jacob himself was given prophetic dreams and visions which came to fruition. And now, confronted with his seventeen year old son's dreams, he was bound to strongly consider the validity of all that was told him by Joseph.

I have never had the Lord come to me in a dream and speak to me or give me clear, prophetic signs of the future. But boy I wish He would! Nonetheless, I am truly thankful that God has made His prophetic Word, the very one we hold in our hands today, as clear as crystal in all sixty-six books. Whenever I need a word from the Lord, I can go to His Word and find exactly what my heart and soul is longing for. I pray that God's Word has the same effect for you. God sustains everything, including us, by His powerful Word (Heb. 1:3). Hold onto His promises to sustain you in every season of your life and

---

[22] Lockyer, Herbert. *Nelson's Illustrated Bible Dictionary*. Pg. 433 , "Gods, Pagan," Thomas Nelson Publishers: Nashville, TN., 1986.

anchor your soul in His truth! You are a dream to me, my friend, thank you for spending time with your Savior today…and with me!

Day Three: One Way Trip

Well, the cat is out of the bag, or should I say, the dreams are on the table! And while we read them yesterday with intrigue, Joseph's brothers rather heard them with envy, disgust, and deceit. Not having been able to speak a kind word to him prior to such an announcement of visions, I am sure at this point, the brothers couldn't even look at him without wanting to punch his lights out! Let's be honest. I think you and I can admit to letting jealousy or envy of another person cause us to avoid them. Maybe you have just seen so and so take one too many vacations or their children in one too many cute outfits and when you scroll through your newsfeed on social media you think, "Seriously, another perfect photo from Mrs. Perfect and her whole perfect family!" Come on' we've all done it! It's amazing how jealousy can turn our hearts away from those individuals who are just as crazy as we are! This is really only one example of ways we can harbor jealousy for others but the result of all forms of envy is the same. It's bitter toxicity invading our bodies. Proverbs 14:30 says, "A heart at peace gives life to the body, but envy rots the bones." Yikes! Sounds like envy is a sure fire way to experience early osteoporosis! But more importantly, envy steals our peace. We cannot be at peace with ourselves, our circumstances, our families, our jobs, you name it…no peace! I confess this hits me right between the eyes today as I feel the conviction of the Holy Spirit reminding me not to envy those who have a seemingly easier or a more fulfilling lifestyle. We have to be so careful not to presume the grass is greener in someone else's yard since we really have no idea what they are experiencing or have experienced in their lifetime. Yes, there are things I wish our family had that other families have and yes, I wish my days were not as difficult or as tiring as they can be, but since I am not living someone else's life, all I can do is focus on the life I have been given and the One who has given it to me. And if I really consider the idea of trading lives with someone else, I panic at the thought of missing out on the intimacy that I have gained with my husband, my children, and most importantly with my Savior! You may still wish you lived someone else's life, especially if you do not have a husband or children or if your husband has abandoned you, but I promise, you will one day be so thankful for everything, the good, the bad, and the ugly. And you will see the way God used everything in your life to mold and shape your character into His likeness.

Let's be honest. I think you and I can admit to letting jealousy or envy of another person cause us to avoid them.

Proverbs 14:30 says, "A heart at peace gives life to the body, but envy rots the bones."

…you will one day be so thankful for everything, the good, the bad, and the ugly.

But let's be real, life is hard. Life has a way of letting us down at every turn. Good thing this life isn't it. Good thing there is an eternal life that we will live which exceeds this life times an infinite number of years. I know Joseph could have found hope in the book of Revelation, had it been written during his lifetime. However, he had his own revelation directly from God in the form of two very specific dreams. Plus he had the verbal promises of God, given to his forefathers, etched deep within his heart. He was going to need all that and more for what he was about to experience over the course of the next ten or so years of his life. Today we will go with him on a long journey. Sadly, we will have to strike his return trip from the itinerary.

According to Genesis 37:12, where had Joseph's brothers gone to graze the flocks?

What did Jacob want Joseph to do (Gen 37:12-14)?

Shechem was located roughly 88 miles north of Hebron.[23] Jacob wanted Joseph to check up on the boys (more like grown men) just as he had done so many times before. Traveling to Shechem could have taken Joseph about a day and a half depending on the terrain and how many times he stopped for a break. Nevertheless, he went on his way, sent from home to seek out his brothers in an area that held some not so favorable memories.

Do you remember, from our study last week, what happened to Jacob's family at Shechem (see Gen 34:1-13)?

Now Joseph was sent to make sure his brothers, who may have had their pictures posted all over the city as, "Shechem's Most Wanted," were not recognized and hung in the city courtyard!

It is quite possible that when Jacob heard that his sons were grazing the flocks Shechem, red flags went up in his mind. He remembered what went down when his sons, Simeon and Levi, murdered every man in the city and then when the rest of Jacob's sons saw all the dead bodies, they carried off the wealth of the deceased, including women and children (Gen 34:25-29). Granted, the boys were provoked to anger by the rape of their sister, Dinah, but we already concluded last week that their revenge was cruel and calculated. Now Joseph was sent to make sure his brothers, who may have had their pictures posted all over the city as, "Shechem's Most Wanted," were not recognized and hung in the city courtyard! There would not have been a way for Jacob to know what was going on unless he sent a messenger and unfortunately no cell phones or even courier mail was available to inform him of his son's status. I just cannot help but image how Jacob felt about these grown sons of his. On the one hand, he cared for them, but on the other, he must have been weighted down by their behavior and inability to be trusted. Again, Joseph was a breath of fresh air and a son whom he could depend on to do what he asked without having to worry about a lack of integrity on Joseph's part.

Do you think Jacob had any clue as to how Joseph might have been treated by his brothers, especially after sharing his dreams with them prior to his being sent out to look for them?

All we know if that Joseph said, "I will go" (Gen 37:13, NASB).

When we read that Jacob sent Joseph off to look for his brothers, our reaction may tend to lean toward asking Jacob, "What were you thinking?!" Or at least that is what I tend to think, but again, we were not there and as much as we study, we still cannot fully grasp the family dynamic, the culture, the frame of mind of Jacob, etc. All we know is that Joseph said, "I will go" (Gen 37:13, NASB). Little did he know he had just agreed to take a journey which turned into more of a suicide mission.

Have you ever embarked on a journey being afraid how things might turn out when you got there? Or worse, you were eager to take a journey and it ended up being the worst trip of your life?

When our little family moved from Seattle to Atlanta, we arrived in Atlanta after a long, tedious flight only to be met with a series of extremely difficult circumstances. My firstborn, Kate, got extremely sick with some sort of stomach flu on the flight and ended up throwing up all over the rental car as soon as we started the engine! Her poor little body remained sick all the way through to the next few days and we wound up in the hospital with her hooked up to an IV. My husband and youngest, Lily Beth, who was a year old at the time, slept in the car in the hospital parking lot. Several other very frustrating situations unfolded in our first few months of the move, which left Sonny and

[23] Lockyer, Herbert. *Nelson's Illustrated Bible Dictionary*. Pg. 1135, "Map 3," Thomas Nelson Publishers: Nashville, TN., 1986.

I looking at each other wondering if we made the right decision by moving to Atlanta in the first place!

When Joseph arrived in Schechem, he may not have been wondering just yet if he had made the wrong decision by going there to find his brothers, but nonetheless, he did find himself wandering.

Who else found Joseph wandering and what did he tell him according to Genesis 37:14-17?

It's hard to say how long Joseph wandered in the open country of Shechem looking for his brothers, but somewhere along the way, he caught the attention of a man who was quite helpful to him. However, when I read this, there is a part of me that wishes we could stop right here and change the story.

If you know what happens when Joseph finds his brothers, how would you change the story at this point?

If I could change the story, I would keep Joseph wandering around in Shechem and coming to the conclusion that his brothers went home. Then I would have had him travel right back home to his father, never having to experience any of the hardship he faced. Oh how I would have messed up the life of Joseph! By trying to keep him from all harm and hardship, I would have greatly stifled the character and calling of one of Israel's greatest heroes! It might seem silly to wish we could change Joseph's story, but I can't help but think of how we tend to want to change the lives of those we love in an effort to keep them from all harm. We ought to never wish for a friend, a loved one, or even a stranger to experience hardship or trials. However, we also need to remember that if we try to step in and change their life story or avert them from the path that God has led them down, we may be doing them more harm than good.

Can you think of an example of getting too involved in someone's life in order to protect them from potential harm or danger?

However, we also need to remember that if we try to step in and change their story or avert them from the path that God has led them down, we may be doing them more harm than good.

Without getting hung up on the obvious things like protecting a child from getting run over or grounding our teenager knowing they are planning on going out and getting into trouble at a party, we were probably able to think of some examples for our last question. Something I thought of was a parent trying to dissuade his or her son or daughter from traveling to a war torn country to do mission work. What about a parent who has bailed their child out of jail for the third time and continues to enable them, preventing the natural consequences of their actions from teaching them valuable lessons? You get the idea, right? Even our prayers or our counsel can prevent someone we love or care about from remaining in God's will and experiencing growth in their character and faith. What about if we are constantly trying to fix up our best friend with blind dates because we are so sad that she is lonely and still hasn't found a husband? First of all, we have no idea how God is working in the depths of her heart, nor does she, or how He is working in the heart and life of the man she may one day marry! If we continue to interfere, we may unintentionally contribute to her marrying the wrong man! Can you imagine?! We must be SO careful in how we pray, participate, and even pity the difficult trials those we care about are facing. Out of love, we do not want to see them suffer, but we also need to be wise how we approach their situation. There may be times we can genuinely offer help and guidance, but we must be sensitive to the Holy Spirit and ultimately seek God's will for their lives. We do not know where God will lead them and how He may use the trial they are facing as a chariot to take them there. The best thing we can do, especially when

We must be SO careful in how we pray, participate, and even pity the difficult trials those we care about are facing.

we do not know what to do, is pray that God's will be done in their lives and that through their difficult situation God will be glorified. We can pray for peace to reign in their hearts and their faith to be strengthened as they wait or as they fight the battle they are engaged in.

Even though we want to rescue Joseph from the inevitable harassment of his brothers, God had a much larger view of how everything would turn out in the end. Beloved, you may be in a situation right now and wonder how in the world any of it could turn out well! Romans 8:28 ought to be a verse we keep in our back pocket for every season, "And we know that in all things God works for the good of those who love Him, who have been called according to His purpose." By looking for his brothers, Joseph was headed straight into a storm that would rage in his life for many years to come. Little did he realize that through all of it, God would work "all things," the good, the bad, and the very painful, together for the good of Joseph. And not only for the good of Joseph, but for the good of thousands of generations after him. Oh sister, God's plans and what He allows in our lives have an eternal impact! We simply cannot see the whole plan yet but we must trust our Heavenly Father. We must trust. We cannot overcome the trials that befall us if we do not trust the Lord to be with us through it all.

Oh sister, God's plans and what He allows in our lives have an eternal impact!

As we end, cry out to God and ask Him to reveal His love so specifically to you in the midst of whatever trial you are currently facing. Ask Him to help you to trust Him and love Him despite what you don't understand. He longs to be with you right where you are. Meet Him there. He loves you and so do I.

Day Four: The Plan, The Pain, The Pit

Well, we couldn't change Joseph's route in yesterday's homework, and sadly we cannot do it today either. But as we concluded, better to leave it be and be further amazed at what God is able to accomplish in and through His children despite dreadful circumstances!

After the man who saw Joseph wandering around looking for his brothers told him where they had gone, he set out on his way to Dothan (Gen 37:17). Joseph had already traveled a significant distance from Hebron to Shechem (over 80 miles) and now he had to go another 13 miles north to Dothan.[24] I am always amazed at how far people in those days traveled on foot through desert regions like Israel! My daughters melt into their car seats after only driving 30 miles in an air conditioned, DVD powered Honda van! They have never been good travelers, but I'm hoping the older they get, the easier it will be, fingers crossed! But in that day, you had no choice but to make your feet the best and most economical form of transportation. Eager to be reunited with his brothers after such a long journey, Joseph finally catches sight of them off in the distance.

So Joseph went after his brothers and found them near Dothan. But they saw him in the distance, and before he reached them, they plotted to kill him (Gen 37:17b-18).

[24] Lockyer, Herbert. *Nelson's Illustrated Bible Dictionary*. Pg. 1135, "Map 3," Thomas Nelson Publishers: Nashville, TN., 1986.

Describe the difference in what Joseph may have been thinking upon seeing his brothers verses what they were thinking when they saw him in the distance.

"Here comes that dreamer!" they said to each other. "Come now, let's kill him and throw him into one of these cisterns and say that a ferocious animal devoured him. Then we'll see what comes of his dreams." Gen 37:19-20

Talk about a stark contrast between the heart conditions of Joseph and his brothers! By the time Joseph sees them he may have broken into a light jog, so glad to finally arrive in their company. Clearly, he had no idea what he was about to run into.

According to Genesis 37:19-20, what was the brother's initial plan for killing Joseph?

Who felt very unsettled by their plot and offered an alternate secret rescue plan (Gen 37:21-22)?

Thank the Lord for Reuben! Last week we touched on the grievous sin that Reuben committed against his father prior to this encounter. Let's look back at Genesis 35:22 and refresh our memory.

What did Reuben do?

Do you think Reuben was trying to show that he felt bad for what he had done to his father in the past by trying to rescue Joseph?

We really don't know anything more about the situation of Reuben sleeping with Bilhah. He may not have done it simply to spite his father. He may have been drunk and may have fallen into temptation and made a really stupid mistake. Nonetheless, we don't read that he apologized or sought his father's forgiveness. Jacob, even at the end of his life, seemed to still be very upset about the whole ordeal, which could have meant he never truly forgave Reuben (see Gen 49:3-4). It's hard to say since we don't have the details but one thing is certain, he was ready to do the right thing when it came to saving Joseph's life!

Have you ever hurt someone so deeply but then were given the opportunity to redeem yourself? How did things turn out? Maybe you are still waiting for an opportunity?

I believe the Lord orchestrates situations that allow us to show those we have unintentionally wounded that we really do want to make things right and are genuinely sorry.

I believe the Lord orchestrates situations that allow us to show those we have unintentionally wounded that we really do want to make things right and are genuinely sorry. Sometimes tangibly doing something in an attempt to redeem our relationships can have a greater impact than our mere words of remorse. Sadly, even though Reuben had a rescue plan in mind, it didn't quite play out the way he had hoped!

What did the brothers do to Joseph when he reached them (Gen 37:23-24)?

The Greek word used for "stripped" denotes a hostile action as the brothers yanked off Joseph's beautiful robe. They took off the most tangible, visible thing which communicated to them how much Joseph was prized in their father's eyes. They hated how much he was loved. When I think about how much God loves us as His children, I can only imagine how much it makes Satan hate us! And not only Satan, but those whose hearts and minds have been blinded from the truth of God's Word and His saving power. Those who have denied Jesus and chosen to live a life in rebellion to Him and those who have chosen to believe a lie in exchange for the truth.

In what way did Jesus say those kinds of people would treat His followers (Matt 24:9, John 15:17-19)?

Then you will be handed over to be persecuted and put to death, and you will be hated by all nations because of Me. Matthew 24:9

We have been chosen out of this world and therefore, we are hated by the world if we are truly living a life in accordance with God's will and way. I think there is some part of us that thinks we ought to be loved by the world because in our hearts and prayers we desire to see people in the world come to Jesus Christ. Where it is our mission to share the love of Jesus with a lost world, there are plenty of people in this world who want to silence Christ by shutting up the mouths of His ambassadors, His children. Although they may not be aware of it, they are aiding in Satan's schemes to prevent the Gospel message from being heard and received. If Satan can just silence us, he will gain tremendous ground in the battle for lost souls! But, we must not be silent! We must not fear the world or Satan, knowing we serve a powerful God who merely has to say the Word, and the enemy will be silenced! Meditate on the following verses and even pray some of them for those whose hearts are hardened toward the gospel and bound by Satan. The first verse is one of my favorites and reminds me to always get my girls singing praise songs around the house!

If the world hates you, keep in mind that it hated Me first. If you belonged to the world, it would love you as its own. As it is, you do not belong to the world, but I have chosen you out of the world. That is why the world hates you. John 15:17-19

IF SATAN CAN JUST SILENCE US, HE WILL GAIN TREMENDOUS GROUND IN THE BATTLE FOR LOST SOULS!

Through the praise of children and infants you have established a stronghold against your enemies, to ***silence the foe and the avenger*** *(Psalm 8:2).*

In your unfailing love, ***silence my enemies****; destroy all my foes, for I am your servant (Psalm 143:12).*

*Jesus said to him, "****Away from me, Satan!*** *For it is written: 'Worship the Lord your God, and serve Him only" (Matthew 4:10).*

I will rescue you from your own people and from the Gentiles. ***I am sending you to them to open their eyes and turn them from darkness to light, and from the power of Satan to God, so that they may receive forgiveness of sins and a place among those who are sanctified by faith in Me*** *(Acts 26:17-18).*

You know what has happened throughout the province of Judea, beginning in Galilee after the baptism that John preached— ***how God anointed Jesus of Nazareth with the Holy Spirit and power, and how He went around doing good and healing all who were under the power of the devil, because God was with Him*** *(Acts 10:37-38).*

Which one of those verses speaks specifically to you this day and why?

God's Word is so powerful and there is nothing, not even Satan, who can stand against it! But we will be hated, we will be persecuted, we will be ridiculed for following Christ. However, if we stay strong and endure, we will overcome with Christ in the end!

Joseph was hated and his brothers, in their hatred, stripped him of his robe and threw him into a cistern.

Describe the scene that comes to mind when you read Gen 37:24?

One of the most important things we can do in order to come out of the pit we have either jumped into or been thrown into, is to recognize where we are in the first place.

The Hebrew word transliterated for cistern in this verse, is *bowr*. Which by its definition means, "a pit hole (especially one used as a cistern or a prison):—cistern, dungeon, fountain, pit, well."[25] Notice the pit Joseph was thrown into did not contain any water and may have been dug specifically for the use of detaining prisoners. How prophetic this pit would be to Joseph's life as the introduction to his coming season of captivity. There are times in our lives where we can trace back and see how a particular incident or maybe a series of incidents began a long season of captivity for us. I know for me, taking my first hit off of a pipe filled with marijuana began for me a quick downward spiral, one I did not recover from for many years. I was given, or rather enticed to try smoking pot just for fun while standing in a circle of my peers in a deserted parking lot at the age of fourteen. Even though marijuana did not become my only method of addiction, it was definitely the key to open a door for several years of recreational drug and alcohol abuse. Then when you add on a heap of unhealthy relationships while under the influence of such vices, the spiral continued and it only took me deeper into a pit of self-destruction and bondage.

We invite others over to visit us in the pit, and sometimes they feel sufficiently enough at home to unpack their bags.
–Beth Moore

What about you? Can you trace an indecent or series of incidents that plunged you headlong into a pit, lasting for several years?

Maybe for you, it wasn't so much something you did on your own, but rather something someone did to you. Maybe it was life that dealt you such a horrific blow and you did not recover…maybe you're still in need of recovery. One of the most important things we can do in order to come out of the pit we have either jumped into or been thrown into, is to recognize where we are in the first place. Beth Moore, in her book, *Get Out of that Pit*, explains what can happen when circumstances early in life dump us headlong into a dusty dwelling.

> Many of us found ourselves in a pit long before we reached Joseph's age of seventeen. To be completely candid with you, I don't even remember life before the pit. I demonstrated behavior patterns of a victim of abuse long before I went to kindergarten. Frequent pit-visiting has a way of turning into pit-living. The earlier we enter the pit or the longer we stay, the more it feels like home. We start hanging pictures on the wall, tidying up the place, and making ourselves comfortable. We invite others over to visit us in the pit, and sometimes they feel sufficiently enough at home to unpack their bags. If we're cool enough enough, we may even move a Pottery Barn couch and Williams Sonoma kitchenware right into the middle of it. But as soon as the rain comes, it all gets soiled. That's the trouble. Every pit has a dirt floor.[26]

[25] "H953 - bowr - Strong's Hebrew Lexicon (KJV)." Blue Letter Bible. Web. 31 Aug, 2016. www.blueletterbible.org.
[26] Moore, Beth. *Get Out of that Pit, Straight Talk About God's Deliverance.* pg 28-29, Thomas Nelson Publishers: Nashville, TN., 2007.

I strongly encourage you to read Beth's book, *Get Out of that Pit*, especially if what she is saying on this topic resonates with you! I have read it several times and can relate all too well with the paragraph you just read above (plus everything else in her book)! We tend to think we are the only ones struggling, the only ones who just can't get it together, but what we fail to notice is that we are in a pit trying to keep our dirt floors clean! It can't happen, my friend, we can't sweep things under the rug and expect to live healthy spiritual lives from ten feet underground! We also are of no use to anyone else when we are pit-dwelling. It's only when we have been brought out of our pit, that we can then look down and see, from a different vantage point, the others who are in theirs. And we certainly cannot help to pull them out of their pits unless we are out of ours!

We ought never to desire for someone to be eternally punished, but it is far better to leave our perpetrators in the hands of the Lord then try to deal with them ourselves.

But what about Joseph?! He was thrown in and there was no quick escape for him in his literal pit! So instead of being delivered out, he was instead, sold out!

As they sat down to eat their meal, they looked up and saw a caravan of Ishmaelites coming from Gilead. Their camels were loaded with spices, balm and myrrh, and they were on their way to take them down to Egypt. Judah, said to his brothers, "What will we gain if we kill our brother and cover up his blood? Come, let's sell him to the Ishmaelites and not lay our hands on him; after all, he is our brother, own flesh and blood." His brothers agreed (Genesis 37:25-27).

"As they sat down to eat their meal…!" Clearly, Joseph's brothers were not at all concerned about what they had just done by throwing Joseph into the cistern. Sadly, those who may have played a major role in our pit plunging seem to go on with their lives completely unscathed. Here we are dying inside and they are leisurely eating lunch, so to speak! Believe me, the Lord notices, and we can trust that if the Lord says, "Vengeance is Mine, I will repay," He will make good on His Word (Romans 12:19b, ESV). We ought never to desire for someone to be eternally punished, but it is far better to leave our perpetrators in the hands of the Lord then try to deal with them ourselves. Pining away at their lack of genuine remorse will only serve to help dig us a deeper hole. And when we forgive, we are not validating the act, but rather releasing the tie that binds us to those who have wronged us. Joseph come to terms with this later, but as for now, he was stuck and had nowhere to turn.

We as Christians, who believe in the true Messiah are already living in the blessed Church era of a risen Messiah, Jesus Christ!

A quick background on the traveling band of gypsies is necessary before we close our lesson for today. The "Ishmaelites" were descendants of Ishmael, Abraham's son whom he bore with Hagar, Sarai's maidservant. Ishmael was older than Abraham and Sarai's biological son Isaac. However, the lineage for the Israelites would begin from Isaac, not Ishmael. God promised to make both the descendants of Isaac and Ishmael into great nations. Yet the promised Messiah would not come from the line of Ishmael but rather from Isaac. I hope I'm not confusing you, but just stick with me. God described back in Genesis 16:11-12, that the descendants of Ishmael would end up becoming a people and nation when He spoke to Hagar, Ishmael's mother, in the desert.

The angel of the Lord also said to her: "You are now with child and you will have a son. You shall name him Ishmael, for the Lord has heard your misery. He will be a wild donkey of a man; his hand will be against everyone and everyone's hand against him, and he will live in hostility toward all his brothers" (Genesis 16:11-12).

What is even more interesting is that descendants of Ishmael are modern day Arabs. The Muslim faith believes that Ishmael is the son whom the Messiah will descend and they are still waiting for his return. We as Christians, who believe in the true Messiah, are already living in the blessed Church era of a risen Lord, Jesus Christ! And we are eagerly awaiting His Second Coming. In the Koran (which is the Muslim Bible), the Muslim Messiah is the Anti-Christ of Revelation and they too are awaiting his arrival which will take place prior to Christ's return.

So I believe it to be no coincidence that the Ishmaelites tried to make a slave out of one of God's patriarchs, Joseph, whom He used not only to save the Israelites (which we will see later) but also to point to the ultimate Savior. This Savior, who would not only bring salvation for Israel but also the whole human race!

How do you see the events of today leading us closer to the return of Jesus Christ, the true Messiah?

Jesus will return one day and the question is not "if," but "when!"

Day Five: A Tragic Report

We ended our lesson yesterday looking into a life-saving twist of fate for Joseph! Yet, you and I both know that with God, there are no coincidences. His brothers were intent on killing him as soon as they saw him approaching them in the distance. Reuben, however, in a moment of conviction, urged the rest of his brothers not to kill him and instead throw him into a cistern. His plan was to go back later and rescue Joseph but another opportunity to be rid of the young dreamer presented itself and the brothers took advantage of it!

Read Genesis 37:25-28 in your Bible and write down the names of the two different descendants of people who were traveling together to Egypt.

So when the Midianite merchants came by, his brothers pulled Joseph up out of the cistern and sold him for twenty shekels of silver to the Ishmaelites, who took him to Egypt. Genesis 25:28

Yesterday in our homework we also discussed the ancestry of the Ishmaelites and now we have mention of Midianites in verse 28. These two groups of people were traveling together and were merchants. The Midianites were descendants of Abraham just as the Ishmaelites. However, instead of having Hagar as his mother, Midian's mother was Katurah. After Sarai died, Abraham married Keturah and they had several sons together. Genesis 25:5-6 tells us that, "Abraham left everything he owned to Isaac. But while he was still living, he gave gifts to the sons of his concubines and sent them away from his son Isaac to the land of the east." So the Ishmaelites and Midianites settled together in the east of Jerusalem, along with many other people groups descending from Abraham's sons. Yet, the only son that Abraham and Sarai had together, Isaac, was the promised child through whom the Lord would bless all nations.

It's safe to say that these traveling merchants, the Ishmaelites and Midianites, were not looking out for the best interest of a young man in distress. Therefore, when Judah saw them approaching their picnic from a distance, he had the bright idea to sell Joseph as a slave.

How much money did the merchants take in exchange for Joseph?

In exchange for a handful of silver, the brother's pulled Joseph right up out of the pit and sent him off to Egypt in the hands of the slave trading merchants. Talk about dirty money! Granted, Judah's idea to sell Joseph was clearly a better option than killing him, but how did he know that Joseph wouldn't die in Egypt or even on the way to Egypt? He didn't. All he thought was that he was averting the responsibility of their direct participation in his death.

We demolish arguments and every pretension that sets itself up against the knowledge of God, and we take captive every thought and make it obedient to Christ. 2 Corinthians 10:5

Do you think this made them any less guilty than killing Joseph themselves?

Jesus, while preaching to a large crowd warned them, "You have heard that it was said to the people long ago, 'Do not murder, and anyone who murders will be subject to judgment,' but I tell you that anyone who is angry with his brother will be subject to judgment…" (Matthew 5:21-22a).

If we confess our sins, He is faithful and just to forgive us our sins and purify us from all unrighteousness. 1 John 1:9

How does this reminder that our thoughts can render us just as guilty as our actions resonate with you today?

It is definitely a sobering reality, one that should have us constantly "taking our thoughts captive and making them obedient to Christ" (2 Corinthians 10:5). I can honestly say that I confess the sin of wrongful thoughts more than my actions, knowing that if I confess my sins, the Lord is faithful and just to forgive me of my sins and purify me from them (1 John 1:9). Our thoughts matter to God and so do our motives.

Are there any hateful, bitter, jealous, sexual, prideful, selfish, doubting or disbelieving thoughts you are harboring right now that you need to confess to the Lord?

WE MAY CHOOSE THE SIN, BUT THE CONSEQUENCES RESULTING FROM THAT SIN CHOOSE US!

Oh my friend, the Lord will put His finger on specific sins in order for us to be cleansed from them. He is not looking to shame or guilt us, but rather purify us and cleanse us in order for us to be free to live in the Spirit, free to honor the Lord with our thoughts and actions.

It is far better to heed the gentle nudge of conviction from the Lord instead of acting out a sin which could hold devastating consequences. We may choose the sin, but the consequences resulting from that sin choose us! Reuben felt that gentle nudge and even planned to help Joseph later, but what he should have done was spoke loud and clear to the brothers desire to kill him in the first place. Instead, he takes off, not exactly sure where he went, but all we know is that when he came back to the cistern, Joseph was gone!

How did he react to the news that Joseph had been sold (Genesis 37:29-30)?

What a bitter end to what began as merely a fit of jealousy among brothers! F.B. Meyer sheds light on how devastating the consequence of their allowing the seed of envy to manifest to such the degree that it did!

> What a genesis of a crime is here! There was a time when the germ of this sin alighted on their hearts in the form of a ruffled feeling of jealousy against the young dreamer. If only they had quenched it then, its further progress would have been stayed. Alas, they did not quench it! Hey permitted it to work within them as leaven works in meal. And "lust, when it had conceived, brought forth sin; and sin, when it was finished, brought forth death" (James 1:15). Take care how you permit a single germ of sin to alight and remain upon your heart. To permit it to do so is almost certain ruin. Sooner or later it will acquire overwhelming force. Treat that germ as you would the first germ of fever that entered your home. At the first consciousness of sin, seek instant cleansing in the precious blood of Christ.[27]

Then they got Joseph's robe, slaughtered a goat and dipped the robe in blood. They took the ornamented robe back to their father and said, "We found this. Examine it too see whether it is your son's robe." Genesis 37:31-32

In bitter anguish of soul, Reuben felt the full weight of guilt for what the brothers had done by selling Joseph. He even "tore his clothes" which was a genuine sign of overwhelming sorrow and cried out, "The boy isn't here! Where can I turn now?" (Gen 37:30) What he was probably thinking was how in the world am I going to explain this to our father! He is going to be absolutely devastated! And telling the truth of what really happened was out of the question. How would they cover up this crime? Well, they did what most people do when found in a tight spot. They lied.

Describe the way they supported their lie with evidence in Genesis 37:31-32.

Frantic to say the least, the men snagged a goat from their father's flock and very likely slit its throat in order to get enough blood to saturate Joseph's beautifully handmade coat. It was the very coat that reminded them of their initial hatred for their little brother. I am sure that no one spoke a word on their long journey back home, each of them imagining in their mind how their father would react to the horrific news they were about to bring him. Upon their arrival home and their delivery of the news to Jacob, their hearts were still hard, particularly in their reference of Joseph as "your son," instead of "our brother." Holding out the bloody tunic they gave these orders to their father, "Examine it to see whether it is your son's robe" (37:32).

What was Jacob's reaction after seeing the bloody tunic (Genesis 37:32-34)?

So his father wept for him. Genesis 37:35b

Can you even imagine his pain! The myriad of feelings, guilt, anguish, sadness, brokenness, emptiness, anger, and horror at the thought of a beast devouring Joseph, all of these emotions must have been surging through him at once! And the guilt mainly derived from the harsh reality that it was he, Jacob, who sent Joseph on the long journey to find his brothers alone! When my family received the news of my little brother's death, my father fell to his knees directly on our hardwood floor in our tiny Seattle home

[27] Meyer, F.B. *Joseph, Beloved, Hated, Exalted.* pg.20-21, CLC Publications: Fort Washington, PA, 2013, ebook.

and wept aloud. He was in anguish. Jacob was in anguish himself, refusing to be comforted.

All his sons and daughters came to him, but he refused to be comforted. "No," he said, "in mourning will I go down to the grave with my son." So his father wept for him. Genesis 37:35

Such a profound realization that our suffering is not in vain but rather becomes a testimony to a lost world!

Oh, what Jacob went through just breaks my heart! And you know the heart of God ached for the beloved patriarch. One day, He too would personally feel the pain of losing a Son in order for a greater glory to be revealed in Him. Suffering is part of the process of our purification and glorification. John Piper sheds light on the incredible truth of suffering in his book *Desiring God* with his commentary on Colossians 1:24.

Now I rejoice in what was suffered for you, and I fill up in my flesh what is still lacking in regard to Christ's afflictions, for the sake of His body, which is the church. Colossians 1:24

> He [Paul] says that it is his own sufferings that fill up Christ's afflictions. This means, then, that Paul exhibits the sufferings of Christ by suffering himself for those he is trying to win. In his sufferings they see Christ's sufferings. Here is the astounding upshot: *God intends for the afflictions of Christ to be presented to the world through the afflictions of his people.* God really means for the body of Christ, the church, to experience some of the suffering he experienced so that when we proclaim the cross as the way to life, people will see the marks of the cross in us and feel the love of the cross from us.[28]

Such a profound realization that our suffering is not in vain but rather becomes a testimony to a lost world! Jacob was in misery but God was working a deeper trust and faith within his soul that he could not have ever imagined.

Hold onto the hope that you profess in Jesus Christ and wait for His deliverance.

Are you hurting, my friend, suffering in various ways that seem to make no sense whatsoever? If so, remember that God is not ignorant of your pain. He is using it and will continue to use our afflictions to bring about a greater glory in us that we simply cannot fathom. The apostle Paul also was the one who said, "I consider that our present sufferings are not worth comparing with the glory that will be revealed in us" (Romans 8:18). Not even worth comparing! Oh, my sister, let that truth bring you hope today! Press hard into your Savior when you experience trials that threaten the very fabric of your being, knowing that whatever you are going through pales in comparison to the eternal hope we have in Jesus Christ! Isaiah 60:20 says, "Your sun will never set again, and your moon will wane no more; the Lord will be your everlasting light, and your days of sorrow will end." They will end one day and when they do, we will no longer remember the depth of our sorrows, but rather bathe in the glory of God's everlasting light!

Jacob would experience joy again one day, but for now, he was in unspeakable pain and it is very likely you may be as well. Hold onto the hope that you profess in Jesus Christ and wait for His deliverance. It will surely come!

Thank you for another wonderful week of digging into God's Word with me! I love you more than words can express and I want you and me to be fully satisfied in Jesus…every day and in every way!

As we close, I want you to pour out your heart to the Lord and thank Him for suffering for you on the Cross. Thank Him for the wonderful Savior that He is and if you are hurting, allow Him to comfort you in your sorrow. I love you, sister.

---

[28] Piper, John. *Desiring God.* pg 269-270. Multnomah Books: Colorado Springs, CO, 2011.

LESSON TWO
The Suffering Son

Few people have had to face more disappointments than Joseph. –Phillips[29]

I. Joseph's ____________ and righteous character propelled his brothers to hate him all the more.

–Jesus entered this world as an innocent babe, as a tender __________ out of dry ground. Isaiah 53:2

–Like Jesus, Joseph was ____________ and _____________ by his brothers. Isaiah 53:3

II. Though sent by his Father, they did not ____________ Him.

–"He came to His own, and those who were His own did not receive Him" (John 1:11, NASB).

III. Before He reached them, they plotted to __________ Him. Genesis 37:18

–"But the Pharisees went out and plotted how they might kill Jesus" (Matthew 12:14).

IV. They __________ Him, then they _________ Him. Genesis 37:23-28

–"...What are you willing to give me if I hand Him over to you?"...(Matthew 26:14).

V. Joseph remained ____________ to his father, despite the high cost!

–"And being found in appearance as a man, He humbled Himself and became obedient to death–even death on a cross!" (Philippians 2:8).

–Joseph's and Jesus suffering was not in vain! Ours isn't either!

–The world's _____________ for us means Heaven's ________________!

---

[29] Phillips, John. *Exploring People of the Old Testament*. pg. 147. Kregal Publications, Grand Rapids, MI: 2006.

GROUP DISCUSSION QUESTIONS:
The Suffering Son

1. From our teaching lesson, in what ways did Joseph's suffering under the hands of his brothers' help you most understand how Jesus suffered under the hands of those who hated Him?

2. Have you ever faced a situation where you were hated by others for your faith in Christ or despised for seeking to live a life of obedience to Christ?

3. Does knowing that both Joseph, Jesus, and countless others in Scripture underwent a time of suffering for their obedience encourage you to persevere in your times of trial and suffering?

4. How do you think Joseph felt after being thrown into a pit and then sold to merchants? How can you relate to some of his emotions in comparison to your own feelings you've experienced in times of hardship or even abuse?

WEEK THREE:
A New Normal

Day One: From Favored Son to Favorite Slave

When I was seventeen years old, my parents signed a waiver for me to enter into the U.S. Air Force. Since I was not yet eighteen, I needed their permission to join. I had just graduated high school and really had no idea what I wanted to do with the next four years of my life, so joining the military seemed like a noble option. When most teenage girls were preparing for college, I was preparing for boot camp. I hadn't really been the military type…ever. But I knew I would cave to peer pressure in college just as I had in high school and would probably just waste time, money, and brain cells if I went. Plus when our very small Montana high school, class of 98', went to a college and career fair in the 4H building, the Air Force recruiter, a young, very attractive man in his uniform, caught my eye right away! And what started out as a bet to go talk to him, ended with me signing the next four years of my life away to the good ole' US of A! I had no idea what I had just gotten myself into! In September of 1998, I got on a plane, flew to San Antonio, TX, and then took a bus to Lackland Air Force Base. I must admit up to that point everything had been rather exciting and fun traveling with new people and all talking about what our first day in boot camp might be like. Well, we really had no idea. When we pulled up, some airmen from the base dressed in their uniforms attended us and kindly shuttled us off the bus. Then they made us stand on a large stretch of pavement under an overhang near the barracks. There were small dots on the ground to stand on so that we could have some uniformity among us. When I look back now, I understand they were trying to get us into what the Air Force calls a "flight" formation. So once we were all situated on our little dots, looking as organized as we could in our civilian gear, we were told to set down our bags. After a few minutes, we heard what would soon become the most terrifying sound for the next eight weeks of our lives… taps. Those little, tiny pieces of metal screwed tightly onto the heels and toes of combat boots striking the pavement with each determined step. And here they came, piercing our ears forcing our bodies to come to attention, and then came the yellin'! I don't think I have ever been yelled at (still to this day) more than I was yelled at in those eight weeks at Lackland, AFB! Those TI's (training instructors) struck a terror in us from day one! Their mission: tear us down and then build us up into a United States Airman, a soldier who willingly took orders and eagerly sought to obey their Commanding Officer. Needless to say, I was shocked and since we are all ladies here, I can tell you plainly that I did not have a bowel movement for two whole weeks! Seriously, all I could think that first night standing on my little assigned spot on the pavement was what in the world had I just gotten myself into!

After a few minutes we heard what would soon become the most terrifying sound for the next eight weeks of our lives... taps.

Seriously, all I could think that first night standing on my little assigned spot on the payment was what in the world had I just gotten myself into!

What about you? Have you been through boot camp or something which had an intense training period and thought what have I gotten myself into?

When I think back to that time in my life, I can't help but imagine that Joseph may have had similar shocked emotions as he was drug even farther away from home by complete strangers who had just purchased him as a slave. And no doubt all he could think of was his father, Jacob, and how devastated he must be knowing his beloved son wasn't coming home. I wonder if he held out hope that his father may come rescue him or his brothers, in a moment of clarity, feel guilty for what they had done, travel to Egypt and buy him back! No such luck. This was it. For the next 13 years, Joseph would not only be separated from his family but also live and work as a slave to Egyptian masters.

Have you ever felt like a slave to your occupation? Maybe a slave to your household duties as a stay at home mom or to an unruly boss, yet you need to keep your job to sustain yourself and your family. What about a slave to a special needs child who you know will never be fully capable of taking care of themselves for the rest of their lives? Or a slave to not being able to fully take care of yourself due to an illness or physical limitation? It could be anything that has made you feel enslaved at some point in your life or currently.

For the next thirteen years, Joseph would not only be separated from his family but also live and work as a slave to Egyptian masters.

Often our lives do not turn out the way we plan. What we thought would bring us joy and utter fulfillment can in itself be the very thing that threatens to enslave us. Such circumstances can either strengthen us or stifle us. We can become subtly bitter. We may not say it out loud but somewhere in the recesses of our hearts, we blame God. Then when we feel too bad for blaming God, we blame the person or situation itself. And when we can no longer blame God or the circumstance, then we blame ourselves. If only I had not taken that job, if only I had not married this man, if only I had made better choices and the list goes on. Where we make the mistake is not necessarily in our choices that brought us to this point, although there are times when we know we were living in sin at the time of the decisions and we clearly did not seek the guidance of the Lord. Yet even in those times, God is merciful to us and does not give us what our sins deserve. Where we wind up making the mistake is in our thought process. We feel enslaved when we don't think that God has anything to do with our situation or circumstances. We are stuck when we forget that we must accept both the easy and the difficult from the hand of the Lord. The devotional, *Streams in the Desert* speaks to the essence of benefiting from our times of captivity allowed by the Lord.

Where we wind up making the mistake is in our thought process.

> If we are to receive benefit from our captivity we must accept the situation and turn it to the best possible account. Fretting over that from which we have been removed or which has been taken away from us, will not make things better, but it will prevent us from improving those which remain. The bond is only tightened by our stretching it to the uttermost.[30]

When we understand that God is well aware of our situation and has, up to this point, allowed things to remain as such, we begin to accept things as they are. We submit. We say something to the effect of, "Lord, if You are okay with this, then so am I." He could change it but if He doesn't, then there is something worth sticking it out for.

Some of us may be facing life-long challenges, others may be more short term but no matter the case, God is the only One who can give us peace in the process. A beautiful

[30] Cowman, L.B., *Streams In the Desert.*, pg 292 , Zondervan, Grand Rapids, MI: 1997, ebook.

thing takes place when we arrive at a state of full submission. We find rest for our souls. We exchange the heavy burden of whatever has threatened or achieved in enslaving us for a much lighter one. Jesus said, "Take My yoke upon you and learn from Me, for I am gentle and humble in heart, and you will find rest for your souls. For My yoke is easy and My burden is light" (Matthew 11:29-30). What an incredible exchange! And since I am no stranger to how difficult it can be to live out this verse in our lives, I have to very tangibly act it out during my times of prayer. One way I do that is to kneel down and pretend that the situation, person, difficulty, whatever it may be, is in my hands and I am placing it before the Lord, pleading with Him to take it from me because it's too heavy. If it's something that is completely overwhelming me, I may have to do that very act for several days, maybe even several times a day. But if I am truly trusting the Lord to exchange my heavy yoke for His lighter one, He will be faithful to do it…in fact, I can trust Him to do it!

Jesus said, "Take My yoke upon you and learn from Me, for I am gentle and humble in heart, and you will find rest for your souls. For My yoke is easy and My burden is light." Matthew 11:29-30.

What heavy burden do you need to exchange today for Christ's lighter one?

Remember the promise that comes through the exchange of burdens; "…you will find rest for your souls" (11:29).

Joseph, no doubt, was weary from his journey to Egypt under his new occupation as a slave in waiting, and was likely in need of a very literal, physical time of rest. Yet it seemed that no sooner that arrived, he was sold to a very wealthy, prominent man.

Read Genesis 37:36 and 39:1. To whom was Joseph sold?

Clearly this man was a good judge of character and could see the strength not only in Joseph's appearance but also his demeanor. The Amplified Bible gives us just slightly more information on Potiphar's position. "…Potiphar, an officer of Pharaoh, the captain and chief executioner of the [royal] guard, and Egyptian…" (39:1, AMP). There is a phrase in there I do not want us to miss and one that will benefit us later. Potiphar was not only captain of the guard but he was also the chief executioner, meaning he had the final say over a prisoner's life. Not to mention he was a high official in the "royal" guard, which means he was often in the company of Pharaoh.

When his master saw that the Lord was with him and that the Lord gave him success in everything he did, Joseph found favor in his eyes and became his attendant. Genesis 39: 3-4a

How does Scripture describe Joseph's role as a slave during his time in Potiphar's household (39:2-6)?

How was Joseph living out Ephesians 6:5-8?

Slaves, obey your earthly masters with respect and fear and with sincerity of heart, just as you would obey Christ. Ephesians 6:5

What an incredible role model is Joseph! I love how Jon Courson simply commentates on Genesis 39:2 as to why Joseph was able to be prosperous even as a slave.

> Why is Joseph referred to as a "prosperous man" even though he is a slave? I suggest it is because, like Paul, he inherently understood that it is not great

gain that brings contentment, but rather contentment that brings great gain (1 Timothy 6:6). Joseph was prosperous because he was content.[31]

Joseph was prosperous because he was content. –Courson

Just as we discussed earlier in today's lesson, our submission to God's sovereign will for our lives gives us rest and enables us to thrive in our current, even slave-like circumstances. So we simply cannot miss that our contentment goes hand in hand with our submission as slaves to Christ. We are to be "like slaves of Christ, doing the will of God from the heart and to serve wholeheartedly, as if you were serving the Lord, not men…" (Eph. 6:6-7, para). This is exactly what Joseph did and it made him and all of Potiphar's household prosper!

From the time he put him in charge of his household and of all that he owned, the Lord blessed the household of the Egyptian because of Joseph. The blessing of the Lord was on everything Potiphar had, both in the house and in the field. Genesis 39:5

Courson enlights us again saying:

> "Whatever you do in word or deed, do all to the glory of God," said Paul (Colossians 3:17). If you, like Joseph, bring the Lord into the situation, your workplace will be blessed simply because you're there… If I were in Joseph's sandals, would I give myself wholeheartedly, enthusiastically, energetically to serving an Egyptian taskmaster–or would I say, "Lord, You've given me dreams and talents and abilities. But they're all being wasted because I'm just a slave?" One of the many things that impress me about Joseph is that he didn't focus on what he lacked, but instead threw himself into the task at hand.[32]

Can you imagine how much we would prosper if we let go of everything that is holding us back from wholeheartedly, enthusiastically, energetically serving our husbands, our children, our co-workers, our bosses, our churches, those both inside and outside of our churches?!

That right there, my sister, is a profound, life-changing, statement! Can you imagine how much we would prosper if we let go of everything that is holding us back from wholeheartedly, enthusiastically, energetically serving our husbands, our children, our co-workers, our bosses, our churches, those both inside and outside of our churches?!

How does what Jon Courson is saying in his commentary convict you in the season you are in currently? To where, what or whom could you use a little more wholehearted commitment?

God is always working to make us more like His Son, Jesus Christ. Imagine if Jesus had held back His enthusiasm and wholehearted commitment to make a way for our salvation through the Cross! Oh Lord, let us learn from Joseph in his time of submission in order to become like You, humble and submissive, even to the point of death. "Humble yourselves in the sight of the Lord, and He will lift you up in due time" (James 4:10).

---

[31] Courson, Jon. *Jon Courson's Application Commentary, Old Testament, Vol 1.* pg. 175. Thomas Nelson: Nashville TN, 2005.
[32] Ibid, pg 176.

Day Two: A Tailored Temptation

When you chose to do this Bible study, did the title stick out to you at all? I'm sure by now the title makes sense after everything Joseph had experienced up to this point in our study! If anyone was misunderstood, it was Joseph. Today will undoubtedly prove the title to be true and once again have us sympathizing with our young man of great character! I will let you in on one of the things I abhor the most and that is being misunderstood. When my intentions are misunderstood, it's one of the worst feelings in the world!

What about you? Have you ever felt misunderstood or maybe even feel that way right now in a certain situation or with a certain person?

When my intentions are misunderstood, it's one of the worst feelings in the world!

It's the worst! When your genuine intentions or actions in a situation are misunderstood or misinterpreted, it can be devastating. This can happen in our homes, our workplace, our circle of friends and even in our churches. And it's often when we are doing the right thing, maybe even the thing God specifically called us to do, that we can feel completely misunderstood by a person or persons involved in our lives. Joseph was no stranger to the very heart ache of being misunderstood.

Think back to some of the ways we have already seen this take place in his life.

Joseph was no stranger to the heart ache of being misunderstood.

Well, pretty much his whole life Joseph's brothers got his intentions all wrong. And is it not usually someone who is jealous of us in some way, shape, or form that misreads all of our actions as selfish or devious! Joseph's brothers certainly felt this way about his favor with Jacob, their father. They also felt this way with his handmade coat, his prophetic dreams, and even his position over them as the chief shepherd. In their minds, he was a spoiled little brat who only deserved death. Yet, as we saw yesterday, even though he was in the position of a head slave, he was more revered by Potiphar's entire household than he was by his own family! In fact, Scripture says that the only thing he, Potiphar, concerned himself with was the food he ate since everything else he fully entrusted to Joseph's care (Gen. 39:6). Joseph played the role of head of the household affairs and it seems that he also looked the part.

How does the last part of Genesis 39:6 describe the way Joseph looked?

By now Joseph had very likely grown into his manhood and as a young, well-built man. He was no doubt handsome. I can also imagine him to have been the strong, silent type with a countenance and character that flawlessly exhibited the leadership qualities he had inherently possessed from a very young age. So with a handsome physique and the position of head of all Potiphar possessed, the other servants of the house were not the only ones who paid close attention to their fearless leader, Joseph!

Who else was taking notice of him (Gen 39:7)?

Goodness! Not only did she take notice, she took action!

What did she want him to do with her?

Talk about a lack of propriety! Clearly, Potiphar's wife was a very straight forward woman, definitely no beating around the bush! We might be able to assume that if Potiphar only concerned himself with the food he ate, leaving everything else in Joseph's care, he may not have concerned himself much with his own wife. She may have felt sorely neglected by the real master of the house and therefore looked to the master of the household affairs for the attention she lacked. Nevertheless, it still didn't give her an excuse to cheat. As women, we must take careful inventory of our personal needs. If we do not feel like we are appreciated, respected, loved, admired, sought after by our husbands, we may think it okay to look for those missing desires elsewhere. And if we are not married, we may look for those needs in the wrong man or woman. Many women have given themselves over to lesbian tendencies because they feel they have been utterly neglected or misunderstood by men. This is deception in its most fleshly form because any relationship that is outside the will of God is a temporary, shallow, vain attempt to pacify needs that can never fully be satisfied. If you feel neglected by your spouse, do not seek companionship elsewhere. If there is a man or has ever been a man that has admired you over your husband, then it was or is a trap set by Satan himself. You must resist the temptation to flirt with the enemy, so to speak. "Resist the Devil and he will flee from you" (James 4:7b)! It's not worth it. I have spoken to countless women who are terribly unhappy in their marriages. One of the first things I tell them is that they must seek full satisfaction in Christ. He must emerge as their true Husband who can meet their needs in a way that no one else ever will. Why the Lord blessed me with a husband that loves me, I'll never fully understand, especially since I did nothing to deserve it! And I mean that, sister, seriously. Nonetheless, I still have very deep needs that even my own husband can never meet. I tell Sonny that I love him very much but there is always going to be another Man that I love more. If I don't make and keep Jesus Christ as my first love, I can't even love Sonny nor could I stay faithful to him. Jesus has got to be the One in whom I find my worth, my identity, my security. We are His bride! "At the resurrection people will neither marry nor be given in marriage; they will be like angels in heaven" (Matt 22:30). So even though our marriage relationships are sacred and intended to even be a picture of Christ and His church, His bride, earthly marriages are not meant for eternity. That is precisely why the Lord wants us to seek Him in order for Him to fully satisfy us and supply all our needs. And when we are seeking Him to accomplish this in us, we are able to give of ourselves to our husbands and other family relationships in a way that is Christ-like and full of grace.

As women, we must take careful inventory of our personal needs.

If I don't keep Christ as my first love, I can't even love Sonny nor could I stay faithful to him.

How do you think your relationship to your husband or your desire to have a husband, if you are not currently married, would change if you truly made Christ your first and ultimate true love?

It means we no longer put our faith in anyone else to satisfy our deepest longings, but rather put our faith in Christ to either change our husbands or bring us one if we are not married.

Making Christ our first love does not mean we entirely lose our desire to be married or our desire for our marriages to get better. But what it does mean is that we are willing to patiently endure seasons with or without a spouse in order to remain faithful and obedient to the Lord. It means we no longer put our faith in anyone else to satisfy our deepest longings, but rather put our faith in Christ to either change our husband or bring us one if we are not married.

Potiphar's wife chose to look to Joseph, a handsome, young man who she thought could satisfy her desires. Although instead of him being compliant with her sensual advances, Joseph reacted in a way she hadn't quite anticipated.

How did Joseph respond to her advances in Gen 39:8-9?

How often did she ask Joseph to go to bed with her (39:10)?

I am amazed at the maturity of Joseph in this account.

I am amazed at the maturity of Joseph in this account. He thoughtfully explained to her his convictions and even respected her enough to tell her why he could not do such an awful thing against God! How easy it may have been for him to give into such strong and daily advances!

Do you think most men today have the same convictions as Joseph did?

I wish we could say they do, but we know better. Sadly, we have heard too many stories of men being unfaithful to their wives, even Christian men. Now don't get me wrong, there are still men out there who are faithful to their wives, but these days, men are bombarded with every kind of sexual temptation known to man! Therefore, it makes it very hard for men not to indulge in some form of sexual immorality. Is looking at porn comparable to cheating on your spouse? In my book it is. And not only in my book is it wrong, but also according to the Bible. Jesus said, "But I tell you that anyone who looks at a woman lustfully has already committed adultery with her in his heart" (Matt. 5:28). Immorality committed in person, in a magazine, on a laptop, on a cell phone…it all falls under the category of unfaithfulness. And not just for men, but also for women! The key to not being overcome with sexual temptation is to know where your allegiance and motivation lies. Joseph had the right attitude, the right mindset, and the right motivation for why he said no to Potiphar's wife. "How then could I do such a wicked thing and sin against God" (Gen 39:9b)? You see, even if his master had never found out about the affair, the Lord would know have known.

Is looking at porn like cheating on your spouse? In my book it is.

How does Hebrews 4:13 remind us that God sees everything?

We tend to think that if no one finds out about our immorality, then it will stay hidden.

We tend to think that if no one finds out about our immorality, then it will stay hidden. Nope. Everything comes out eventually, even if it's before the judgment seat of Christ! And honestly, it's better for us to come clean now instead of waiting until then! The Lord is forgiving and merciful and promises us that, "If we confess our sins, He is faithful and just and will forgive us our sins and purify us from all unrighteousness" (1 John 1:9). However, we must not continue in sin and presume upon the grace and mercy of Christ.

Joseph stayed strong in the Lord and resisted temptation. Nevertheless, Potiphar's wife took her advances one step further and tried to take Joseph to bed by force!

One day he went into the house to attend to his duties, and none of the household servants were inside. She caught him by the cloak and said, "Come to bed with me!" But he left his cloak in her hand and ran out of the house. Genesis 39:11-12

Flee the evil desires of youth, and pursue righteousness, faith, love, and peace, along with those who call on the Lord out of a pure heart. 2 Timothy 2:22

Ponder for a moment Joseph's reaction to the woman's strong and final advances. Did his actions line up with Scripture according to 2 Timothy 2:22 and 1 Corinthians 10:13?

No temptation has seized you except what is common to man. And God is faithful; He will not let you be tempted beyond what you can bear. But when you are tempted, He will also provide a way out so that you can stand up under it. 1 Corinthians 10:13

Notice how Joseph did not stay in her presence and try to resist her by merely standing still. We cannot forget that Joseph was a man and had impulses just like any other man. However, more than human impulse, Joseph had strength of character. That, my friend, can override the lustful passions that we all possess in our fleshly, sinful nature. I imagine that very few men would have been able to resist the temptation of Potiphar's wife. Yet we read how Joseph respected her by first explaining why he could not sleep with her. Now we see him run away from her in order to maintain his integrity and right standing with not only Potiphar, but with the Lord!

Sadly, Potiphar's wife was too blinded by the lusts of her flesh to understand the harsh implications of her next move.

What was her next move after Joseph ran away (Gen 39:13-18)?

Goodness gracious! If I were Joseph, the only thing I would have said at that point would have been, "Seriously!?" After all he had been through already, now this? Scripture does not tell us if Joseph was even given the opportunity to defend himself. Sadly, I think not. However, instead of shaking his fist at God and blaming Him, Joseph stayed calm. Psalm 37:7 says, "Be still before the Lord and wait patiently for Him; do not fret when people succeed in their ways, when they carry out their wicked schemes." Being misunderstood and wrongly accused may often result in difficult consequences. Yet, it is far better for us to be still before the Lord and wait for His deliverance than to turn away from Him in bitterness and anger. Clearly Potiphar's wife lied, first to the servants under Joseph, then to her husband. Such deception! She even referred to him as "the Hebrew slave you brought us…" (39:17). She was set on being intimate with him and then she harbored resentment and hatred for him. Even if Joseph had given her what she wanted, it's very likely she would have either viciously blackmailed him or eventually decided to blow their cover. Yet despite the gross misunderstanding and maligning, Joseph's conscience before the Lord was clean, therefore the Lord continued to bless his obedience.

Yet, it is far better for us to be still before the Lord and wait for His deliverance than to turn away from Him in bitterness and anger.

Joseph's master took him and put him in prison, the place where the king's prisoners were confined. But while Joseph was there in prison, the Lord was with him; He showed him kindness and granted him favor in the eyes of the prison warden. Genesis 39:20-21

No matter the outcome, our eyes look to the Lord who is favorable to those whose hearts are pure before Him.

Day Three: From Potiphar's Wife to Prison Life

My two girls, Kate and Lily Beth love watching Curious George. My oldest, who is now eight, loved that little monkey so much that when she turned two, we threw her a Curious George birthday party! If you are not familiar with the PBS TV cartoon, it's all about the adventures of a little monkey and his owner whose name is "the man with the yellow hat." George, the monkey, gets into all kinds of mischief in every episode. After watching the show, Sonny used to always say that the man in the yellow hat had to be a fictional character because there is no one on earth who could have that much patience with a crazy monkey without eventually sending it back to the jungle, dead or alive! Yet, there is part of me that imagines Joseph being like the man in the yellow hat or yellow turban! Even though we do not know exactly how he reacted to all the sheer chaos ensuing around him, he must have remained calm enough to earn quite a respectable place even in prison. If I were him (which would be strange I know) I would be in the corner of my jail cell crying. It would be one endless pity party that I would throw for myself every day. But not our man Joseph! It seemed like he fought depression with perseverance. He was certainly not numb to his feelings, which we will see more evidently later on in our study. Nonetheless, he did not allow himself to be put to shame by the very complex, very perplexing circumstances he faced. Neither did he let them dictate his ability to press on.

It seemed like he fought depression with perseverance.

Why was he able to press on and keep working hard despite all he had been through (Gen 39:23)?

THE LORD WAS WITH HIM!

THE LORD WAS WITH HIM! I know I just gave you the answer in all caps but if we would only believe the truth of this verse for ourselves! We are not alone, sister! Joseph felt the very presence of God reassure him with every step, every misunderstanding, every heartache, every trial, and every difficulty. The Lord was there and there to stay!

Do you think you would experience more rest and less anxiety if you truly and confidently believed the Lord was always with you?

"For I know the plans I have for you," declares the Lord, "plans to prosper you, not to harm you..." Jeremiah 29:11

"...so are My ways higher than your ways, My thoughts higher than your thoughts." Isaiah 55:9

I know I would! I wish I could say that I was always a hundred percent confident the Lord was with me, but sometimes when the heat is turned up in the trial that is currently visiting my doorstep, I forget and I worry. And honestly, maybe I don't worry so much that He has forgotten me but I worry about what He might allow to happen or not happen in a given situation.

Do you ever feel that way? Try to think of an example of when you worried about what God might allow to happen or not to happen in a difficult situation.

One thing I try to do when I am worried about how a situation may turn out, is meditate on God's character. I remind myself of how God loves me unconditionally and wants to prosper me and not harm me. I think about how faithful He is and has always been to me. I ponder how He gave His life for me and that I can trust the Man who died for me.

The Lord Himself goes before you and will be with you, He will never leave you nor forsake you. Do not be afraid; do not be discouraged. Deuteronomy 31:8

But when He, the Spirit of truth, comes, He will guide you into all the truth… John 16:13

I also think about how much higher His ways and thoughts are than mine. Plus, when I consider His mercy and grace, I know that no matter what happens, He will never leave me nor forsake me. You see, my friend, I ponder His Word, His truth, His promises to me in Scripture and that is how I pull myself out of a super funk of despair and depression. Actually it's not me pulling myself out, but rather the Holy Spirit of God, who lives inside of me and who reassures me through the very Word of God that I can trust His ways. Deception and lies from the enemy threaten my confidence and tempt me to only focus on my current circumstances. In order not to succumb to the enemy's schemes, the Holy Spirit (who guides us into all truth) sheds light on the lies and brings me out of the darkness of despair and into the marvelous light of God's glory and goodness.

Do you meditate on God's Word when you are in a spiritual, mental, or emotional funk? It's okay to be honest if you don't.

The goal is not to beat ourselves up for not doing it but rather be reminded that we should do it! I struggle too! Sometimes I need others, like my husband or a good friend to speak words of truth to me when I am too overwhelmed to seek it for myself. Graciously, the Lord will use many ways to encourage us with His Word if we will just listen. He is our helper, He is in fact "our refuge and strength, an ever-present help in trouble" (Psalm 46:1).

What are you going through right now and could use His ever-present help?

Let's be honest, sometimes we forget to ask the Lord for help. We get caught up in the situation and we forget to take it before the Lord, our Helper. We forget He is with us (closer than we could ever imagine) and waiting for us to turn things over to Him.

Joseph was not immune to the heartache of being misunderstood but evidently he was learning the secret of strength by looking to his Helper. And instead of ranting and raving over the injustice done to him, he remained calm and steadfast. That's where he found his strength, "…in quietness and trust is your strength…" (Is. 30:15).

His quietness and trust in the Lord earned him the favor not only of the Lord, but also of the prison warden.

Who granted Joseph favor in the eyes of the prison warden and what did the warden place Joseph in charge of (Gen. 39:21-22)?

Joseph was given a tremendous amount of responsibility in prison. With Potiphar being the captain of the guard, it is presumable that Joseph was well known by many of Egypt's administrators. And it's also possible that Potiphar's wife had a reputation of her own, therefore the warden felt sympathetic to his plight. Just speculation on my part, but plausible considering Joseph's integrity. And even though Potiphar "burned with anger" upon hearing his wife's allegations against Joseph, his conscience may have haunted him since he had only ever experienced the utmost loyalty from his chief servant, Joseph (39:19). However, there was no way Potiphar could believe the pleas of a Hebrew servant over his wife's accusations, even if it was Joseph. Potiphar's hands were tied, yet he was still the overseer, (the captain of the guard) meaning he was the main boss of the prison where he placed Joseph. Therefore, it's very likely that the prison warden did nothing without Potiphar's approval. It's possible that after some time, Potiphar informed the prison warden that Joseph could be trusted and that he was an exceptional worker. Whether that idea came from the warden's own observations or if Potiphar gave him the insight, he was brought to the place where he "...paid no attention to anything under Joseph's care..." (39:23). It seemed the warden wasn't worried Joseph would escape nor was he afraid to give him full access to the prison in order to maintain its many precarious duties. A genuine, determined, single minded, full of integrity and sound judgment kind of young man is very hard to come by...even in that era.

Because of my integrity You uphold me and set me in Your presence forever.
Psalm 41:12

Do you know anyone whose character and integrity are similar to Joseph's?

Let us not become weary in doing good, for at the proper time we will reap a harvest if we do not give up.
Galatians 6:9

Hard working, self-motivated people who can be depended upon are of great value to their employer. And to think that Joseph maintained this level of dedication even in prison! "It is not so important *what* we do as *how* we do it. The motive that inspires us is the true gauge and measure of the worth or importance in our life," says Meyer.[33] Joseph's motives stayed pure. What a test of character for this young man! He had no idea what the Lord was preparing him for but he took each step of his journey, even the dark and discouraging ones, with courage and endurance. "...if we are faithful to forge ahead and 'if we do not give up' (Gal 6:9) someday we will know that the most exquisit work of our lives was done during those days when it was the darkest."[34] Just ponder that truth, dear friend. What are you facing or what have you faced? When you want to just throw your hands in the air and say, "I quit," would you dare to believe that the Lord is working things in your heart, your character, and your life that are going to last for eternity? Galatians 6:9 is a promise that I feel the Lord has etched into my soul and I hold tight to it when the dark days come and I feel as though I just can't put one foot in front of the other. I believe there were days when Joseph felt extremely weary and felt like giving up. But he kept pressing on and he didn't even have the Scriptures as we do!

"It is not so important *what* we do as *how* we do it. The motive that inspires us is the true gauge and measure of the worth or importance in our life," says Meyer.

Is there a situation you are currently in where you feel like giving up?

You may feel like giving up on a rebellious child, on an unloving spouse, on a dead end job, on a friend or family member, on being a mom, on being a teacher, or on life itself. Like the prophet Elijah, we may be ready to say or have already said, "I have had enough, Lord...take my life; I am no better than my ancestors" (1 Kings 19:4). Yes, he said that because he was completely and utterly exhausted mentally, emotionally, and spiritually and ready to throw in the towel! Yet instead of throwing in the towel, he threw himself upon the mercy of God. That is exactly what we must do when we are ready to give up on

Yet instead of throwing in the towel, he threw himself upon the mercy of God!

[33] Meyer, F.B. *Joseph, Beloved, Hated, Exalted.* pg.29, CLC Publications: Fort Washington, PA, 2013, ebook.
[34] Cowman, L.B., *Streams In the Desert.*, pg 326 , Zondervan, Grand Rapids, MI: 1997, ebook.

something or someone, knowing the Lord would rather us stick with it or stick with them! Similar to Joseph, we may have to tough it out in a horrible situation and make the best of it. We may need to cry out as the prophet Jeremiah and say, "Lord, you have seen the wrong done to me. Uphold my cause!" (Lam. 3:59). Joseph could have prayed that same prayer (as Jeremiah did many years later) when considering all the wrong that had been done to him by his brothers and Potiphar's wife. Yet the Lord was upholding Joseph's cause through every injustice done to him. As Meyer explains, "They may have stripped him of his coats, but they couldn't strip him of his character!"[35]

Do you trust the Lord to uphold your cause in situations where you feel wrongly accused or misunderstood?

When the Lord takes pleasure in anyone's way, He causes their enemies to make peace with them. Better a little with righteousness than much gain with injustice. In their hearts humans plan their course, but the Lord establishes their steps. Proverbs 16:7-9

Read Proverbs 16:7-9 in the margin. How does the Lord work on behalf of those in whom He takes pleasure?

We may not feel justified today, tomorrow, or even in this lifetime. However, the Lord is on our side and is working things together for our good, no matter how bleak our situation. He can make our enemies be at peace with us, He can restore us, reaffirm us, and continue to establish every step we take along our journey here on earth. So keep walking, my friend, the darkness will dawn, what He says, He will do and will not leave undone!

Day Four: The Butler & the Baker

"Oh Lord, make me like this man whose integrity, motivation, and conviction exhibit the utmost purity!"

As I open my Bible for today's lesson, I am astounded at the sheer beauty and authenticity of Scripture. We are living in a generation where the preaching and teaching of God's Word is no longer the main emphasis in many churches today. This just absolutely breaks my heart because how in the world are we going to know who God is and what He requires of His people unless we know what He says in His Word! Many new believers today are being cheated out of true discipleship, where they ought to be taught Biblical truth and disciplines of the faith. We will talk more about this later in our study but let me just say one thing and that is how truly overjoyed I am that you are investing your time and your heart into this study! You are being a faithful student of God's Word and you will be blessed, my sister, yes, you will be blessed. I have already been blessed by Joseph's life more than words can express. I have found myself begging the Lord to infuse in me the character of Joseph. I have prayed, "Oh Lord, make me like this man whose integrity, motivation, and conviction exhibit the utmost purity!"

In what ways have you found yourself wanting to be like Joseph?

[35] Meyer, F.B. *Joseph, Beloved, Hated, Exalted.* pg.26, CLC Publications: Fort Washington, PA, 2013, ebook.

Joseph was a rare find, but for us who possess the Holy Spirit of God, we too can have a character like this young man. We must be willing to let the Spirit have His way in our lives and weed out anything from our flesh that is preventing us from changing. Ultimately, we want to take on the very character of our Lord Jesus Christ. Joseph reflected the image of Christ more than most. "Joseph learned, hundreds of years before our Savior taught it from the Mount of the Beatitudes, the blessedness of the pure in heart," says Meyer.

Placed in a dungeon, Joseph spent years sleeping in a damp, dark, isolated cell with his feet clad in iron.

Though pure in heart, nevertheless he suffered, as did our Lord. Placed in a dungeon, Joseph spent years sleeping in a damp, dark, isolated cell with his feet clad in iron. Though he was given the liberty of running the prison by day, it was the darkness that must have felt overwhelming. And as we continue to read of the next encounter for Joseph, we read that it happened, "Sometime later…" (Gen. 40:1a). It had been roughly eleven years since he was thrown into the pit by his brothers and now Joseph was a young man of twenty-eight. How many years he spent in Potiphar's house verses Potiphar's dungeon are not clear. But, we know it was more than two years since he remained confined until the age of thirty and had already been there for "some time." Nevertheless, the arrival of two unsuspected inmates no doubt brought a glimmer of hope to his long suffering soul!

Read Genesis 40:1-4 and describe Joseph's new inmates and where they were placed.

The two officials, the butler (cupbearer) and the baker were very important men who served in Pharaoh's palace. Wycliffe's Bible Dictionary gives us an informative description of the role specifically of butlers (or more namely cupbearers) in Scripture.

> Pharaoh's "butler" was a cupbearer (Gen 40:1-41:13). Solomon had cupbearers (1 Kings 10:5; 2 Chron 9:4). The only cupbearer mentioned by name is Nehemiah, cupbearer to Artaxerxes (Longimanus, in Nehemiah 1:11). His first duty, described in Nehemiah 2:1, apparently involved responsibility to guard against poison in the king's cup, perhaps even to tasting it first himself. Hence, the king's life lay in his cupbearer's hands who, obviously, would be a trusted man, and presumably of high rank and able to advise the king in matters of state.[36]

For Pharaoh to be angry with his chief cupbearer, he must have either given bad advice or forgotten to take a sip of his master's night cap!

We can see that the cupbearer didn't just simply serve the king a drink but literally put his own life on the line every time Pharaoh became thirsty! That honestly sounds like a terrible occupation to me! Talk about a high stress job! And not only did he test the waters, so to speak, but he also gave the king advice in matters of state. For Pharaoh to be angry with his chief cupbearer, he may have either given bad advice or forgotten to take a sip of his master's night cap! Scripture doesn't tell us what he did wrong but it must have been bad enough to land him in prison. The baker was also a very important man but rather than give counsel, he kept to the kitchen. Wycliffe also enlightens us on this common occupation of Biblical times.

> Egyptian bakers are known to have made as many as 38 varieties of cake and 57 of bread. They were compelled to render strict accounts of their supply of materials to their lord's overseer of granaries… Dough was prepared by mixing flour with boiling water then kneading. A small piece of yesterday's dough was crumbled into the water before

[36] Pfeiffer, Charles F., Vos, Howard F., Rea, John, *Wycliffe Bible Dictionary.* pg. 1227, "Cupbearer." Hendrickson Publishers, Inc: Mass, 2001.

mixing to act as yeast or leaven. Baking was done in one of three ways. The most primitive method was to make a fire over large flat stones, and cover with ashes (1 Kings 19:6). A second way was to bake the dough on a griddle or pan (Leviticus 2:5; 6:21; 1 Chronicles 9:31; 23:29). A fire was built in a pit to form hot coals over which the griddle was placed (Isaiah 44:19). The most desirable method was to use an oven with coals in the bottom from a fire made the night before.[37]

After reading the descriptions of these interesting occupations, which one would you rather be if you had to choose between the two? Cupbearer or Baker?

We may have both picked the baker! However, as we study further, we may change our minds! It seems that the position of the cupbearer was more prominent if not more dangerous. Although we are not certain how either of these men offended Pharaoh, it could be that the baker neglected to render a strict account of his supplies (as we read in Wycliffe's commentary above). Or if that wasn't the case, he might have just made a bad batch of cinnamon rolls for breakfast! It's hard to say but whatever he did must have been offensive enough to land him in the cell next door to his co-worker, Mr. Cupbearer of the palace. And speaking of prison cell, I find it so interesting how Scripture describes the prison in Genesis 40:3 saying, "…and put them in custody in the *house* of the captain of the guard, in the same prison where Joseph was confined" (italics mine). Remember the "captain of the guard" was Potiphar. So his house and the prison could have been one in the same, kind of like a house and its basement. Except it may have been more like Potiphar's palace and his lower dungeon level.

The captain of the guard assigned them to Joseph, and he attended them. Genesis 40:4

Why do you think Potiphar assigned the two new felons to Joseph?

It must have been difficult for Joseph to continually see Potiphar, even taking orders from him, yet with the knowledge that he had been wrongly accused by him and his wife. It makes me sick to my stomach to think about how misunderstood Joseph must have felt! Nonetheless, loyal Joseph stays obedient! Again we see Joseph flawlessly living out Ephesians 6:5, "Servants be obedient to your masters according to the flesh with fear and trembling, in singleness of your heart, as unto Christ." Potiphar knew he could trust Joseph (even after all the accusations) because he knew Joseph was an obedient servant!

Do you see yourself as a servant or more as someone who would rather be served?

Do you see yourself as a servant or more as someone who would rather be served?

I know that's kind of a tough, straight forward, possibly even convicting question! But don't worry, it convicts me too. I have to ask myself this question often, especially when I feel entitled to certain things or when I get tired of serving my family and feel like they need to reciprocate! We may feel that way at our jobs, in our churches, with our family or even with our friends at different times. Or it may be that we feel we could use an occasional, "thank you," a spa certificate, a house maid service, or just someone noticing how much we do for everyone else around us. You may have someone in your life that notices your hard work and shows their appreciation in very tangible ways. But there may be some of us who do things and it seems no one notices. In those times, we must remember who we are ultimately serving and that He sees our good deeds and hard work.

[37] Ibid, pg 1223, "Baker."

Jesus used an example of giving to the poor to describe the attitude in which we should go about doing good deeds in Matthew 6:3-5. How are we to serve others according to these verses?

We live in a society and culture that shares everything on social media! It's hard not to want to tell the world via picture, video, or crafted message what we are doing for Jesus and for others. But if we truly wanted to be rewarded by the Lord, according to Matthew 6:3-5, we would keep those things a secret. Even the amount of money we give in our local churches or to Christian organizations should be something we do not discuss with others. If we considered our acts of service sacred to the Lord, then we would not feel entitled to being rewarded by anyone other than Him. That could bring us a lot of freedom if we find ourselves running into seasons of bitterness over the endless tasks we have been assigned. It could also remind us that it is better to serve than to be served. Of course, Jesus would never ask us to do something that He Himself had not already perfected.

Of course, Jesus would never ask us to do something that He Himself had not already perfected.

Instead, whoever wants to become great among you must be your servant, and whoever wants to be first must be your slave— just as the Son of Man did not come to be served, but to serve, and to give His life as a ransom for many. Matthew 20:26-29

Jesus was a fully submissive servant to God the Father and He also served others with the utmost compassion. We see this same, Christ–like compassion in Joseph.

Read Genesis 40:4-7 and describe the way Joseph inquires of their downcast state in verses 6-7.

The two officials of Pharaoh had already "been in custody for some time," and therefore would have known Joseph, their attendant, quite well by this point in our text (40:4b). On one particular morning, Joseph, doing his morning rounds, possibly bringing breakfast or making sure everyone was awake, noticed something different about the countenance of the butler and the baker. "Why are your faces so sad today?" asked Joseph (40:7). I love the fact that he noticed! He cared about how they were feeling and didn't assume that they were dejected or depressed merely because they were in prison! Both of these men, whose dreams greatly disturbed them found consolation in their attendant Joseph. Goodness, I knew I liked this guy!

Therefore, as God's chosen people, holy and dearly loved, clothe yourselves with compassion, kindness, humility, gentleness and patience. Colossians 3:12

How can we emulate this characteristic of compassion according to Colossians 3:12?

Don't you just love the visual of "clothing ourselves" with these Christ–like virtues as described in Colossians! Joseph may not have had his coat of many colors, but he still had his heart of many virtues.

Out of the virtues described in Colossians 3:12, which one do you feel you wear the best?

We won't go through the pain of highlighting which one we wear the worst but what we can do is pray that if we are lacking patience (that's mine), the Lord would graciously supply us with an extra layer! I can get so impatient with myself, my husband, my children, and my dog (he's still a puppy and has a very small bladder, so he still tinkles in the house…a lot!). I guess I could throw in the need for gentleness, especially when Charlie (our pup) can't quite hold it! Okay, I need to be reminded to clothe myself with just about all of these virtues on a daily basis! The Lord knows we are not perfect, but He is.

The Lord is ready to supply us with everything we need through the power of the Holy Spirit, if we will simply ask.

What do you need to ask for today?

The more we come to terms with how needy we are, the more we will find our needs supplied by our Father. It's His will for us to be so dependent on Him that we ask for His indwelling power to help us get through the day and to love others with the same level of compassion that He loves us. I know it's hard and I know there are days where we feel like an absolute failure. But since Christ doesn't give up on us, we can't give up on Him, nor can we give up on ourselves to be changed little by little, in order to reflect the character of Jesus.

The more we come to terms with how needy we are, the more we will find our needs supplied by our Father.

Joseph reflected the character of Christ and took an interest in the welfare of others. We saw it first with his brothers as he made the arduous journey to find them and now we see it as he inquired of these two men whose hearts are downcast. Even though many details of Joseph's life are unaccounted for in Scripture, we can imagine that there were many people whose lives Joseph took a genuine interest in from the time he was young up to where we find him now.

As we end our lesson today, ponder some ways you can serve others. It may be a family member, a co-worker, a neighbor, or a stranger. Also, practice serving in silence and allowing the Lord to be the only One looking upon your acts of compassion with His loving approval. Lord, make us more like You and let us only be concerned with gaining Your approval. Thank you, my sweet friend, for your transparency and vulnerability to this study and for being in these pages with me because we want to be more like Jesus! Love you!

Day Five: Distressing Dreams

Yesterday's homework showed us Joseph's compassionate side as he paid careful attention to those whom he attended in Potiphar's prison. Two men in particular, the butler (cupbearer) and baker woke up quite distressed after each having very peculiar dreams.

"We both had dreams," but there is no one to interpret them..." Genesis 40:8

If you are a dreamer, what is the strangest dream you have ever had? How did you feel when you woke up?

I rarely remember my dreams, but there have been those occasions where the dream I was having was so vivid, I had to wake myself up just to get out of it. Sadly, I think it's the nightmares rather than the nice, peaceful dreams that I seem to remember for several days after having one. Wycliffe's Bible Dictionary sheds some light on the strange phenomena of dreaming in its following definition.

Dreams can also be caused by powerful stimuli or suggestions and emotions which may be pleasant or unpleasant.
–Wycliffe's Bible Dictionary

> A dream is a series of images or thoughts occurring during sleep. When these are unpleasant the cause is sometimes a physical disorder. Dreams can also be caused by powerful stimuli or suggestions and emotions which may be pleasant or unpleasant. These need not be of recent occurrence but can lie

> buried in the subconscious for a long period and, even though apparently forgotten by the individual, can make themselves felt in disturbing dreams.[38]

I know that there are probably a gazillion definitions out there for dreams and many people who have studied them in depth, but at least this definition gives us some insight into how our emotions can feed our dreams, which I find very interesting! As far as interpretations, I do know people who have had dreams where they felt the Lord speak to them, but I have never had one of those. I wish I did! Dreams ran in the Patriarch's family. Nelson's Bible Dictionary validates at least two instances where the interpretation of dreams was required, one of which we are already familiar.

> Two special cycles of dreams in which expert interpretation was involved occur in the Old Testament. The first cycle related to Joseph (Gen 37:5-10), or his officers. The second cycle involved Daniel (Dan 2:14-45), with dreams coming to Nebuchadnezzar of Babylon. The dreams in each case pertained to events of the future. God granted the ability to interpret these dreams to Joseph (Gen 40:8, 41:12) and Daniel (Dan 2:20-45).

The Lord not only gave His chosen people dreams but He also gave pagan people dreams throughout Scripture. We already read how Joseph was given the ability to interpret his own dreams back in Gen 37:5-10, but now the Lord gave him the ability to interpret the dreams of Pharaoh's officials. The same is true for the prophet Daniel as he was enabled by the Lord to interpret the dreams of Nebuchadnezzar, King of Babylon.

I love Joseph's humility! It's so refreshing!

Who did Joseph say all interpretations of dreams belong to, according to Genesis 40:8?

I love Joseph's humility! It's so refreshing! Never do we read of Joseph taking credit for anything. Even after interpreting his own dreams at the age of seventeen, he still does not turn the attention on himself or say to these officials that he alone can interpret their dreams for them. What a relief it must have been for these men to offload their distressing dreams with the hopes of Joseph, by the power of God, being able to interpret them!

Okay, let's have a little fun here for you visual learners! The cupbearer is the first to tell his dream so go ahead and read Genesis 40:9-11 and draw an image of his dream. Don't stress and if you absolutely hate to draw, instead, just write it down in your own words, if you prefer.

"This is what that means," Joseph said to him. "The three branches are three days. Within three days Pharaoh will lift your head and restore you to your position, and you will put Pharaoh's cup in his hand, just as you used to do when you were his cupbearer." Genesis 40:12-14

Such great news for Mr. Cupbearer of the palace! I'm sure the baker, also listening intently was eager to hear such a promising interpretation of his dream. Oh, how I wish I could see your drawing! I'm a terrible artist so if you didn't even attempt, don't worry at all. Some of us are just going to forever be stick figure kind of artists! That's me!

---

[38] Pfeiffer, Charles F., Vos, Howard F., Rea, John, *Wycliffe Bible Dictionary*. pg. 474, "Dream." Hendrickson Publishers, Inc: Mass, 2001.

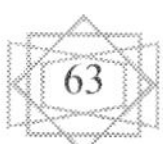

After giving him such a favorable interpretation of his dream, Joseph then asked the cupbearer to do something very important for him in return.

What did he ask him to do in Genesis 40:14?

"Remember me…" (40:14) seems like such an easy thing to do in light of the attention Joseph had given to both of Pharaoh's officials. We'll see if he followed through! And yet, here we also have the first words spoken by Joseph in his own defense to the cupbearer. "For I was carried off from the land of the Hebrews, and even here I have done nothing to deserve being put in a dungeon" (40:15b). You go, Joseph! Finally we hear him speak his heart like a normal mortal man. He didn't deserve any of what had been done to him and even though he remained obedient to the Lord, you know he still didn't wish to be in the situation he was in. Later, he would understand the "why" but right then he saw an opportunity for someone to potentially aid in his freedom and he took it. What is so interesting is that the same word used earlier in our text for "pit" is the same Hebrew word used here in 40:15 for "dungeon." Joseph didn't deserve the first pit and he definitely didn't deserve the second one! He was ready to tell someone, whether or not he was heard.

When the chief baker saw that Joseph had given a favorable interpretation, he said to Joseph, "I too had a dream…" Genesis 40:16a

Do you ever just feel like saying, "I don't deserve this!?"

Sometimes we don't even realize we've become bitter until God so mercifully exposes the sin in our hearts.

Its okay for us to tell someone that we feel like life has been unfair to us! Where we run into trouble is if we live with a chip on our shoulder and become bitter toward the Lord. Sometimes we don't even realize we've become bitter until God so mercifully exposes the sin in our hearts. This happened so vividly to me last year when I was sitting having some quiet time with the Lord one morning. I had been very discouraged over my circumstances at the time and I couldn't stop crying. The Lord got my attention by speaking to my heart and asking me if I blamed Him for my struggle. Feeling humbled and humiliated, I said,"Yes, Lord, I guess I do blame You!" Broken, I confessed my sin to Him and He restored me, reminding me that even though He had the power to change everything, He was still working within the framework of my current state. He was teaching me things that I would learn no other way unless I stayed right where I was. What felt like a mess to me was really what He was using to deepen His message of mercy and grace in my life, teaching me truths I couldn't learn without being in the exact circumstances I was in. The same was true for Joseph. Meyer says that talking with political officials, such as the butler and baker "would have given him great insight into political parties and knowledge of men and things generally, which in later days must have been of great service to him."[39]

What felt like a mess to me was really what He was using to deepen His message of grace and mercy in my life, teaching me truths I couldn't learn without being in the exact circumstances I was in.

Are you up for another attempt at one more drawing because we still have one more dream to look at! Again, don't do it if you hate the idea! You will find your next dream assignment in Genesis 40:16-17.

[39] Meyer, F.B. *Joseph, Beloved, Hated, Exalted.* pg.45, CLC Publications: Fort Washington, PA, 2013, ebook.

"This is what that means," Joseph said. "The three baskets are three days. Within three days Pharaoh will lift off your head and hang you on a tree. And the birds will eat away your flesh" Genesis 40:18-19.

Yikes! Talk about a huge upset! Joseph's interpretation for the baker was instead a death sentence. I wonder if the baker regretted even asking Joseph about his dream in the first place. He was probably desperately wishing and hoping that what Joseph had foretold would not come to pass. I know I would be! The Amplified Bible give us a little more graphic interpretation of the bakers fate in 40:19 saying, "Within three days Pharaoh will lift up your head but will have you beheaded and hung on a tree, and [you will not so much as be given a burial, but] the birds will eat your flesh." Again, terrible news! The baker must have really done something awful to receive such a sentence.

!

Looking back at the text, what was the occasion which took place three days after Joseph's interpretations of the dreams (Genesis 40:20)?

How did things turn out for the cupbearer and the baker in 40:21-22?

He restored the chief cupbearer to his position, so that he once again put the cup into Pharaoh's hand, but he hanged the chief baker, just as Joseph had said to them in his interpretation. Genesis 40:21

What a celebration Pharaoh's birthday must have been! I find it so interesting that he wanted to take care of his judicial duties on his birthday. When it's my birthday, I don't want to do anything that requires decision making unless it's decide where we should go out to eat or what kind of cake we should have! It could have been that he was ready to have his chief cupbearer back for the big day and thought he might as well get them both out of prison together. It's hard to say, but one thing is certain…Joseph was right! More importantly, the Lord was faithful and allowed Joseph to interpret the dreams exactly how they turned out.

After his day of redemption, did the chief cupbearer make good on his promise to Joseph (Genesis 40:23)?

Sadly, he did not. Seriously?! Chief C, what was the deal?! Couldn't you have remembered Joseph for crying out loud! That's what I think I would have said to him had I been there. But of course, I wasn't. Can you even begin to imagine how discouraged Joseph must have felt? The glimmer of hope that he may be set free seemed to go out as quickly as it was lit. Talk about a roller coaster of emotions that Joseph lived through those thirteen years from pit to pit! Oh, but how God had a plan! Joseph just couldn't see it yet and he was still in training. God was still molding and shaping his character for what He was planning on doing with him later on. His time just hadn't come yet. This is why good ole' chief cupbearer didn't remember. Not because he was just absent minded, but because the Lord wasn't ready for Joseph to meet Pharaoh yet. He still had two more years before he would step out from within those prison walls (Gen. 41:1a). If you've been waiting for God to move in your life or to move you and He hasn't done it, don't lose hope! Like I've said before, if you are still drawing breath, there is still time for there to be a move of God in your life. What is much more important is what the time of waiting and suffering is accomplishing in our lives. Calling upon the Amplified Bible again, let the following verses burrow deep into your being now that we have truly come to know the sufferings our beloved Patriarch, Joseph.

…he was laid in chains of iron and his soul entered into the iron… Psalm 105:18

…and He sent a man before them–Joseph, sold as a slave. His feet they hurt with fetters; he was laid in chains of iron and his soul entered into the iron, until his word [to his cruel brothers] came true, until the word of the Lord tried and tested him. Psalm 105:17-19, Amplified Bible

Let this phrase of that verse soak in for a moment, "...he was laid in chains of iron and his soul entered into the iron..." His sufferings became part of who he was. They made him the man that God needed for the calling He was placing upon his life. But we see a second very important phrase there also, "...until the word of the Lord tried and tested him." The "iron," the prison, was working in him but so was the testing of the Lord to see whether or not Joseph would remain faithful to his God. Joseph had to trust that his dreams as a young boy of being exalted to a position of power were still part of God's foreordained plan. "Now faith is being sure of what we hope for and certain of what we do not see" (Hebrews 11:1). Our faith is never more exercised than when every circumstance around us begs us to disbelieve the greatness of our God. Faith is not being certain of the outcome but being certain of how mighty and all powerful is our God! I know I have quoted Meyer over and again but his wisdom and depth is just too good to miss when considering the gloriously humbling truth of Psalm 105:17-19.

God wants iron saints; and since there is no way of imparting iron to the moral nature except by letting his people suffer, He lets them suffer. -Meyer

> *It is just this that suffering will do for you. The world wants iron fists, iron sinews, and muscles of steel. God wants iron saints; and since there is no way of imparting iron to the moral nature except by letting his people suffer, he lets them suffer. "No chastening for the present seemeth to be joyous, but grievous; nevertheless afterward it yieldeth the peaceable fruit of righteousness unto them which are exercised thereby" (Heb. 12:11). Are you in prison for doing right? Are the best years of your life slipping away in enforced monotony? Are you beset by opposition, misunderstanding, censure and scorn, as the thick undergrowth besets the passage of the woodsman pioneer? Then take heart; the time is not wasted. God is only putting you through the iron regimen. The iron crown of suffering precedes the golden crown of glory. And iron is entering into your soul to make it strong and brave.*[40]

Oh, I wish we didn't have to suffer! I wish Christ had never had to suffer on the Cross! I wish sin had never entered into humanity from the disobedience of Adam and Eve. I wish, I wish, I wish...! But praise the Lord, there will be an end to our struggles and what seems to be working against us, God is using it to work for us! Life is hard. Life is unfair. It hurts and we bleed. But God is good. He knows the way we take, He hears us and He is for us. I am sobbing right now as I write all of these words because one day, my dear friend, we will see our sweet Jesus face to face and we will forget all our sufferings in light of His glorious presence. One day. And what a day that will be!

...one day, my dear friend, we will see our sweet Jesus face to face and we will forget all our sufferings in light of His glorious presence.

[40] Meyer, F.B. *Joseph, Beloved, Hated, Exalted.* pg.46, CLC Publications: Fort Washington, PA, 2013, ebook.

LESSON THREE
The Misunderstood Man

To be misunderstood even by those whom one loves is the cross and bitterness of life –Amiel.[41]

I. Joseph ____________ and ______________ difficult temptation presented to him by Potiphar's wife (Gen. 39).

> *–Watch and pray so that you will not fall into temptation. The spirit is willing, but the body is weak (Matt. 26:41).*
> *– No temptation has overtaken you except what is common to mankind. And God is faithful; He will not let you be tempted beyond what you can bear. But when you are tempted, He will also provide a way out so that you can endure it (1 Cor. 10:13).*

II. Jesus _____________ His temptations from the devil by proclaiming the ____________! (Matt. 4:1-11).

> –________________ come to _______________ our character and calling (Matt. 4:3, 8-9).
>
> *–Then Jesus was led by the Spirit into the desert to be tempted by the devil (Matt.4:1).*

III. Joseph was misunderstood by his ___________, ___________, & ____________.

IV. Jesus was misunderstood by the ____________ He served, His ___________, and the ___________ sect.

> –He was ________________ (Matt. 9:23-26).
> –He was ________________ (Matt. 12:1-14).
> –He was ________________ (Matt. 12:22-28).
> –He was ________________ (Matt. 14:15-21 and Matt. 15:32-39).

V. Yet when the opportunity came to _______________ Himself, He ______________ (Matt. 27:11-14).

---

[41] Cowman, Charles E. Mrs., *Springs in the Valley*. pg. 391. Zondervan Publishing House: Grand Rapids MI., 1997, Kindle Version.

GROUP DISCUSSION QUESTIONS

The Misunderstood Man

1. How does Joseph's and Jesus' example of staying strong in the face of temptation encourage you to stay strong when you are faced with temptation?

2. Have you ever been accused of wrongdoing, as Joseph was with Potiphar's wife, and had to face consequences despite your innocence?

3. Do you ever struggle with serving the Lord when others around you misunderstand or ridicule your actions or motives, as they did Jesus'? How can Jesus' example of perseverance help you to keep going despite the opposition?

4. When given the opportunity to redeem His reputation, Jesus chose to be quiet instead. How can we get to a similar place of confidence in our reputation with God, instead of worrying so much of what others think of us?

WEEK FOUR:
From Pits to Palace

Day One: Two Full Years

It's a staggering and sobering thought that from the last verse in Genesis 40 to the first verse in 41, two full years had passed for Joseph and he was still in prison. Lord knows we feel like we have been in there with him by this point in our study! I know I have! And if you, my sister, are in prison right now, you can relate all too well! I've tried with all my might to envision Joseph's face and every detail of the prison which held him for so many years. I've cried at the thought of what he endured. I've cried over the fact that he was so grossly misunderstood. You know that even though the Lord had allowed such suffering to befall him, it still hurt the heart of the Father to see one of his sons go through such a difficult stretch.

When two full years had passed... Genesis 41:1

Do you ever stop to consider that our present sufferings, even though the Lord has allowed them, make the heart of our Father ache for us?

One very specific instance we see this happen is when Jesus found out that Lazarus had died (John 11). When Jesus heard the news of his passing, He wept (John 11:35). He wept, even though He knew He would, in a few moments, raise Lazarus from the dead! The Lord cares and feels so deeply for us, more than we could ever image! With each discouragingly passing day, the Lord cared and sympathized with Joseph's plight. Yet, with an all–knowing perspective, God saw and anticipated the very night that would begin to rattle the chains right off of Joseph's feet!

Just briefly describe what happened in Genesis 41:1-7 by writing a short description of Pharaoh's dreams under each category:

Pharaoh had a dream...He fell asleep again and had a second dream... Genesis 41:1, 5

Cows:

Heads of Grain:

These dreams seem to come in twos! Joseph had two dreams, then he interpreted two dreams in prison, and now Pharaoh is having two dreams! Interesting how the Lord brought all that about! Maybe He sent the second dreams to confirm the first. We will find our answer to that question later in today's reading. Nonetheless, Joseph was about to really feel the effects of his God given ability to interpret Pharaoh's dreams verses the four previous ones.

In the morning his mind was troubled, so he sent for all the magicians and wise men of Egypt. Pharaoh told them his dreams but no one could interpret them. Genesis 41:8

Troubled by his dreams, who did Pharaoh send for as soon as he woke up (Genesis 41:8)?

I wonder how long it took for each of those pagan, worldly men to try and figure out what Pharaoh's dreams meant. What I would have given to be a fly on the wall, hearing some of the interpretations they tried to come up with, yet remained stumped! One of the men present at the dream interpretation rally that morning was our good ole' Mr. C. Remember that the chief cupbearer who not only held Pharaoh's cup but was also an advisor to him? Amidst the flurry of elegantly dressed men, wielding their magic eight balls and chanting their petitions to their false gods, one man, possibly deep in thought, perks up and says, "Today I am reminded of my shortcomings!"

What I would have given to be a fly on the wall, hearing some of the interpretations they must have tried to come up with, yet they remained stumped!

Then the chief cupbearer said to Pharaoh, "Today I am reminded of my shortcomings. Pharaoh was once angry with his servants, and he imprisoned me and the chief baker in the house of the captain of the guard. Each of us had a dream that same night, and each dream had a meaning of its own. Now a young Hebrew was there with us, a servant of the captain of the guard. We told him our dreams and he interpreted them for us, giving each man the interpretation of his dream. And things turned out exactly as he interpreted them to us: I was restored to my position, and the other man was hanged. Genesis 41:9-13

You could have heard a pin drop. Just picture Pharaoh's hand, pulling on his beard, listening intently to his advisor tell the only story that seemed to make sense all morning. There he sat, thinking back to his birthday two years ago and the truth of what he was hearing coming from the mouth of his cupbearer as he held his morning orange juice (we can pretend). Then maybe even looking back at the motley crew of magicians and so–called wise men who were also staring in amazement at what all they too had heard Mr. C say! Quickly and defiantly standing to his feet, maybe he pointed straight to one of the palace corridors and said, "Go now! Get me this Hebrew man since none of you numb skulls can tell me anything! Maybe he can interpret these disturbing dreams!"

How did Joseph prepare himself to meet with Pharaoh (Genesis 41:14)?

Joseph was not your average Joe. He knew he was probably sporting a real funk being down in the dungeon all these years and refused to walk among Egypt's civilized patrons looking haggard and scraggly. Plus he knew that this was a God ordained opportunity to present himself as "one approved, a workman who does not need to be ashamed and who correctly handles the word of truth" (2 Timothy 2:15). If the word of truth needed to be spoken, Joseph was the only man in all of Egypt who could do it. Yet, he remained humble enough to give the credit directly to God, even bypassing himself as the middle man. And there he stood, shackles off his feet, clean shaven, dressed in clean clothes, bright eyed in the light of day and breathing in the air above his previous dungeon dwelling. He was free. Did he know for how long? No. But at least for that one morning, after thirteen long years of being a servant and a prisoner, Joseph stood with all the power of Heaven and earth behind him, in the presence of Egypt's King Pharaoh.

Yet, he remained humble enough to give the credit directly to God, even bypassing himself as the middle man.

Pharaoh said to Joseph, "I had a dream, and no one can interpret it. But I have heard it said of you that when you hear a dream you can interpret it." Genesis 41:15.

How did Joseph respond to Pharaoh in Genesis 41:16?

The King James Version of Genesis 41:16 says, "And Joseph answered Pharaoh, saying, *It is* not in me: God shall give Pharaoh an answer of peace." Oh I love that! "It is not in me!" What are you facing today where you find yourself saying, "I don't have it in me!" Let me tell you something...you don't have to! We are supposed to put aside "self" and depend on God to do whatever He wants to do in us and through us!

Now may the God of peace, who through the blood of the eternal covenant brought back from the dead our Lord Jesus, that great Shepherd of the sheep, equip you with everything good for doing His will, and ***may He work in us what is pleasing to Him****, through Jesus Christ, to whom be glory for ever and ever. Amen. Hebrews 13:20-22 (emphasis mine).*

If anything, our job is to stay empty in order to be filled!

"May He work in us...!" And not only that, look at the phrase before, "equip you with everything good for doing His will..." We are not supposed to have it "in us" apart from the Holy Spirit of God. If anything, our job is to stay empty in order to be filled! And what are we to stay empty of? Self! Philippians 4:7 in the NASB says of Jesus, that He, "...emptied Himself, taking the form of a bond-servant..." The KJV says, "...made Himself of no reputation and took upon Him the form of a servant..." Boy, don't we live in a world of people today who want to make a reputation for themselves! Christian and non–Christian alike! Rather than look to Christ as our example, we would rather look to the world and then tag a Jesus label on it. But thankfully we see Joseph, full of Christ–like humility standing before Pharaoh as a true bond–servant of the Lord saying, "I cannot do it, but God will give Pharaoh the answer he desires" (41:16, paraphrase mine). Jon Courson draws a beautiful parallel to the life of Jesus and Joseph's response to Pharaoh.

Those who are successfully used by the Lord are those who cause people to say, "God is good," without taking any credit for themselves.
–Jon Courson

> Like Joseph, Jesus continually drew attention to His Father. "Let your light shine before men that they will glorify your Father," He said (Matthew 5:16). That is why you'll never read about people glorifying Jesus. You see, Jesus was able to minister in such a way that people would see the light, but glorify the Father. Those who are successfully used by the Lord are those who cause people to say, "God is good," without taking any credit for themselves.[42]

If we want to see God do powerful things in our midst, we must be willing to get out of the way and let Him have His way!

Ah! So good! What a wonderful example in Joseph and Jesus for us to emulate! "God opposes the proud but shows favor to the humble... Humble yourselves, therefore, under God's mighty hand, that He may lift you up in due time" (James 4:6, 1 Peter 5:6). The way up is down; down on our faces before God! That way when He does lift us up, we are not prideful and arrogant, trying to do things on our own instead of continually surrendering ourselves to the Lord's leading in our lives. If we want to see God do powerful things in our midst, we must be willing to get out of the way and let Him have His way!

In order to let the Lord have His way and speak through Him, Joseph first listened intently as Pharaoh explained both of his dreams to him.

Read over the dreams again in Genesis 41:17-22 as he explains them to Joseph.

I find it interesting that Pharaoh's account of his dreams contained a few added details and some emphasis on how bad the cows really looked and how very withered and thin

---

[42] Courson, Jon. *Jon Courson's Application Commentary, Old Testament, Vol 1.* pg. 179. Thomas Nelson: Nashville TN, 2005.

and scorched the head of grain really were! It's kind of like my husband and I telling the same story but my details and facial expressions make things sound much more dramatic than when he tells the story! I know, you are probably thinking, "You, Laura? Dramatic? No way!" I know, I'm just misunderstood for being dramatic, no truth to it at all! If this were a text, I'd attach one of those emojis with the crying laughing face and add a big LOL! You don't know how many times I've wanted to attach an LOL (laugh out loud) to the majority of the sentences I have written throughout our study! But I refuse to do it because this is a Bible Study, not a text! LOL! Okay, no more LOL's! Plus if you are like me, you probably receive about a million texts a day and need to sit down with Bible, paper, and pen, phone turned off and take a mini "vaca" from your world of cellular distraction! Age of Information and globalization…who knew it would make our brains so tired and eyes so bugged out on technology! Alright, enough of all that, back to the ancient world and the much anticipated interpretation…

Then Joseph said to Pharaoh, "The dreams are one in the same. God has revealed to Pharaoh what He is about to do. The seven good cows are seven years, and the seven good heads of grain are seven years; it is one and the same dream. The seven lean, ugly cows that came up afterward are seven years, and so are the seven worthless heads of grain scorched by the east wind: They are seven years of famine. It is just as I said to Pharaoh: God has shown Pharaoh what He is about to do. Seven years of great abundance are coming throughout the land of Egypt, but seven years of famine will follow them. Then all the abundance in Egypt will be forgotten, and the famine will ravage the land. The abundance in the land will not be remembered, because the famine that follows it will be so severe. The reason the dream was given to Pharaoh in two forms is that the matter has been firmly decided by God, and God will do it soon. Genesis 41:25-32

Sounds like good news and bad news all rolled into one! Seven good years but the seven bad years will be so bad that the good ones preceding it will be long forgotten! And remember what we talked about earlier, how the dreams came in twos? Well, at least in this instance we see that "the reason the dream was given to Pharaoh in two forms is that the matter has been firmly decided by God, and God will do it soon" (Genesis 41:32). After Joseph interprets the dream, he may have paused for a minute and waited for Pharaoh to respond but there was only silence. So then Joseph continued, offering a God–sent remedy to the prophetically terrifying famine that was just pronounced upon Egypt.

What was that remedy according to Genesis 41:33-36? Just briefly summarize in your own words.

We may experience times of famine in our lives, but the Lord will sustain us.

Oh what a true reminder that God always supplies His grace in our times of greatest need! He provides salvation for the most desperate of souls, scorched and withered by the effects of sin. To those who have seemingly had the best years of their lives swallowed up by a myriad of wrong choices and endless regrets. To the weak and heavy laden, He says come, buy food that will satisfy your soul and store up for yourselves treasure in Heaven that nothing on this earth will destroy. We may experience times of famine in our lives, but the Lord will sustain us.

God had a plan to sustain, not only the citizens of Egypt, but the surrounding towns and cities as well. His plan involved putting a discerning and wise man in charge of the land of Egypt as it's governor (41:33), then having Pharaoh also "appoint commissioners over the land to take a fifth of the harvest" during the seven years of abundance (41:34). Then they were to store the grain collected during abundance, holding it in reserve for the country during the seven years of intense famine (41:36). This plan seemed good to Pharaoh!

The plan seemed good to Pharaoh and to all his officials. So Pharaoh asked them, "Can we find anyone like this man, one in whom is the spirit of God?" Genesis 41:37-38

Wouldn't you love to have that be said of you! "Can we find anyone like this woman, one in whom is the spirit of God?" If we want this to be true of us, we have to ask ourselves if we are willing to suffer and be tested by the word of the Lord, just as Joseph was, in order to be seen as someone in whom is the spirit of God? We can say all day long that we are filled with the Holy Spirit, and that may be very true, but do others see that in us? Or do we look and act like everyone else, Spirit and non–Spirit filled alike? So what sets us apart, what makes us look different? One thing that sets us apart these days is knowing, studying, and believing God's Word. Also, living in obedience to the Word and not wavering from the truth of the Gospel will really make us an odd ball in today's generation! Taking a stand for God's Word may very well isolate us from the main stream, even main stream Christianity, but was Joseph constantly surrounded by friends and family as a slave in Potiphar's house or prison? No. He was alone and willing to remain standing alone with His God even if no one else stood with him. That's the kind of iron saint our God is looking for. Are you willing to stand alone in order to let Him make you an iron saint? I know I want to! I pray you do too, friend!

Taking a stand for God's Word may very well isolate us from the main stream, even main stream Christianity...

Also, living in obedience to the Word and not wavering from the truth of the Gospel will really make us an odd ball in today's generation!

Day Two: Egypt's New Governor Zaphenath–Paneah

What a whirlwind of a day for Joseph as he stepped out of the prison and into Pharaoh's palace, never to return to prison again! Truly from rags to riches! And to the extent of those riches, well we will find out today!

Then Pharaoh said to Joseph, "I hereby put you in charge of the whole land of Egypt." Genesis 41:41

What did Pharaoh do after telling Joseph such incredible news (41:42-43)?

The first thing Pharaoh placed on Joseph was his signet ring. Such a ring was used to authenticate a document by making a distinctive design in clay or wax when pressed down onto it.[43] In essence, the ring sealed the document. Pharaoh knew his new governor

...and men shouted before him, "Make way!" Genesis

[43] Pfeiffer, Charles F., Vos, Howard F., Rea, John, *Wycliffe Bible Dictionary*. pg. 1540, "Seal, Signet." Hendrickson Publishers, Inc: Mass, 2001.

would need to have the authority to authenticate documents. Also, having this ring would validate Joseph's authority to anyone who felt the need to dispute it. Then Pharaoh dressed him in robes of fine linen and put a gold chain around his neck (41:42). Let's just think here for a moment of how resplendent this is of our salvation in Jesus Christ. If we have been truly saved, we experienced Jesus lifting us up out of the dungeon of sin of our past life, placing His seal upon us by giving us the Holy Spirit, then clothing us in His righteousness, and promising us a crown of glory to wear for all eternity! What a beautiful picture of grace!

What a beautiful picture of grace!

A beautiful scene indeed was the clothing and honoring of Joseph in the midst of all of Egypt's highest officials. Then Pharaoh takes the opportunity to show off his new right hand man throughout the streets of Egypt.

He had him ride in a chariot as his second-in-command, and men shouted before him, "Make way!" Thus he put him in charge of the whole land of Egypt. Genesis 41:43

What do you think Joseph was thinking as all of this was taking place?

Hmm…overwhelmed?! If I were him I may have thought I was having another dream of which I would wake up and have to interpret later! He must have been thinking, "Is this really happening?"

Have you ever had the Lord just blow your mind with an answer to your prayers that was so far beyond what you were expecting…in a good way?!

Just as He parted the Red Sea, one day the Lord will say, "Make way!" to the very circumstances that are preventing you from seeing His plan unfold!

I am sure we can both recall some serious blessings that just left us in awe! For some of us, we may still be waiting on the Lord to deliver us or give us one of the main desires of our hearts. All I have to say to that is don't lose heart, don't give up. Keep waiting and trusting the Lord to come through. Remember, Joseph thought he had been forgotten by the cupbearer and maybe even some days by the Lord, while he was in prison. Yet the Lord did not forget Joseph and He has not forgotten you, my sweet friend. Don't lose heart. Just as He parted the Red Sea, one day the Lord will say, "Make way!" to the very circumstances that are preventing you from seeing His plan unfold!

Then Pharaoh said to Joseph, "I am Pharaoh but without your word no one will lift hand or foot in all Egypt. Genesis 41:44

What new name did Pharaoh give Joseph and who was the woman that became his wife (Genesis 41:45)?

Try saying that name several times! The pronunciation is zăf̍ năth-på-nē`å and has several meanings such as, "Nourisher of the land of the living one," "the giver or nourishment of the land," and later the Jews interpreted it as "the revealer of secrets." However, one of the most common meanings for this name is "the god speaks and he lives."[44] I love that last interpretation of his name because that is what happened and continues to happen…God speaks and He lives! Isn't it just absolutely surreal that the same God who gave Joseph the interpretation of Pharaoh's dream is the same God we

[44] Pfeiffer, Charles F., Vos, Howard F., Rea, John, *Wycliffe Bible Dictionary*. pg. 1833, "Zapthnath-Paaneah." Hendrickson Publishers, Inc: Mass, 2001.

worship today! He is the same God who speaks and lives in the hearts of all His children! He is the same God who created the entire universe and holds everything together! He is the same...yesterday, today, and forever. Just take a moment to thank Him and praise Him for how truly awesome He is!

You know Joseph was thanking the Lord and probably still in shock, especially when he realize that he not only had a new name but also a new wife!

Who was his new wife's father (Genesis 41:45)?

Asenath's father was believed to be a pagan priest of the Egyptian sun-god Re` or Ra in On (the Greek Helioplis).[45] I'm sure he was an interesting father–in–law! There were many pagan priests and idols in Egypt. Even the Nile River was worshiped by the Egyptians. The Nile god, Hapi, represented life and nourishment and even in Pharaoh's dreams he sees himself standing by the Nile, possibly paying homage as he had many times before.[46] That's why it's so fitting that Pharaoh gave Joseph the name Zaphenath-Paneah with one of its meanings being "the giver or nourishment of the land!" It was Joseph, by the power of His God, who was the one nourishing the people, not Hapi, the god of the Nile, during the severe famine.

It was Joseph, by the power of His God, who was the one nourishing the people, not Hapi, the god of the Nile, during the severe famine.

Even though he still worshipped false gods, the Pharaoh in Joseph's time seemed to be much more calm and sensible, especially to the Hebrew people than other Pharaohs of the Bible. Think about the Pharaoh during Moses time who wouldn't let the Hebrew's go. He wasn't a very reasonable guy! Archeologists believe that the Pharaoh during the time of Joseph was named Sesostris and that he also had a prime minister or vizier (governor) named Mentuhotep, which is believed to have been another name given to Joseph during that time.

> Sesostris is known to have had a vizier, or prime minister, by the name of Mentuhotep who wielded extraordinary power, and some scholars have identified this vizier with the biblical Joseph. Sir Alan Gardiner assigns a date of 1971–1928 B.C. to Sesostris I, but by a revised chronology he would have been ruling when Joseph was sold as a slave into Egypt in about 1681 B.C... A graceful canal runs from the River Nile to bring water into the Faiyyum Oasis. It is known as "Joseph's Canal" and was dug during Dynasty 12, possibly at Joseph's orders in preparation for the expected famine.[47]

Joseph's life made a dramatic mark in history! At thirty years old, thirteen years after being sold as a slave that terrible day by his jealous brothers, here we see a man, full of wisdom and wielding extraordinary power. His schooling for the position was certainly harder than your average PhD! What strength of character and determination this man possessed after such a school of suffering!

Joseph collected all the food produced in those seven years of abundance in Egypt and stored it in the cities. Genesis 41:48

Briefly describe how he executed his plan to save Egypt from the severe famine in Genesis 41:46-49.

Joseph worked hard, just as he had from the time he was a young man. Everything that the Lord had foretold through Pharaoh's dream came to pass.

---

[45] Pfeiffer, Charles F., Vos, Howard F., Rea, John, *Wycliffe Bible Dictionary*. pg. 1383, "Potipherah." Hendrickson Publishers, Inc: Mass, 2001.
[46] Ibid, pg 1206, "Nile."
[47] Down, David & Ashton, John. *The Glorious Middle Kingdom*. September 24, 2009. https://answersingenesis.org/archaeology/ancient-egypt/the-glorious-middle-kingdom/.

During the years of abundance, no time was wasted gathering food and storing up huge quantities of grain. Remember back in Potiphar's house how the Lord blessed everything Joseph did, "From the time he put him in charge of his household and all that he owned, the Lord blessed the household of the Egyptian because of Joseph" (Genesis 39:5). It looks like that blessing continued as we read that, "Joseph stored up huge quantities of grain, like the sand of the sea; it was so much that he stopped keeping records because it was beyond measure" (41:49). The Lord blessed Joseph at home with his father, in Potiphar's home, in prison, and then as governor over all Egypt! Even in the hard times, the Lord never left him. Joseph remained faithful in small things and difficult things, therefore the Lord could entrust him with greater responsibility in the greater, more challenging things.

"Whoever can be trusted with very little can also be trusted with much and whoever is dishonest with very little will also be dishonest with much." Luke 16:10

How did Jesus speak of that same concept of faithfulness in Luke 16:10?

We may feel like we deserve more responsibility or a greater position within our sphere of influence but the Lord is looking at what we are being faithful in right now. Can we be faithful in our homes, faithful in a job that is much less than what we had hoped for, faithful serving the Lord in a much less honorable position than others? It's not about what we are doing as much as it's about how we are doing the very task that has been assigned to us. Joseph is such an outstanding example for us to model when it comes to that since everything he did, he did it well no matter what or where it was! As we have said so many times before...he possessed genuine integrity!

Not only was the Lord blessing Joseph's new career as Pharaoh's second–in–command, but He was also blessing his family.

Before the years of famine came, two sons were born to Joseph by Asenath daughter of Potiphera, priest of On. Joseph named his firstborn Manasseh and said, "It is because God has made me forget all my trouble and all my father's household. The second son he named Ephraim and said, "It is because God has made me fruitful in the land of my suffering." Genesis 41:50-52

I want you to underline the meanings of the names of each of Joseph's sons.

...For the past troubles will be forgotten and hidden from My eyes. "See, I will create new heavens and a new earth. The former things will not be remembered, nor will they come to mind." Isaiah 65:16b-17

What three things did Joseph consider to be great blessings in his life according to these two names?

Isaiah 65:17 just resounds in my thoughts as I ponder how Joseph was feeling when he named his sons. "The former things will not be remembered..." The Lord had done such a new and glorious work in Joseph that even he was amazed at how he was able to not dwell on the past pain of his youth. He even needed to forget how much he missed his father's household in order to be present in his new calling in Egypt. Then when he named Ephraim, Joseph was able to see the benefit of his time of suffering. This too reminds me of Peter's words, under the inspiration of the Holy Spirit, in *1 Peter 1:6-7.*

In this you greatly rejoice, through now for a little while you may have had to suffer grief in all kinds of trials. These have come so that your faith–of greater worth than gold, which perishes even though refined by fire–may be proved genuine and may result in praise, glory and honor when Jesus Christ is revealed.

Right now we may be in the "suffer*ing* grief in all kinds of trials" stage. We may not yet be able to see past the struggle as Joseph did when naming his sons. But take heart, my dear one, "these have come so your faith…may be proved genuine…" When we are in the midst of the refining fire, struggling in ways that seem unfair or just down right terrible, we must take on the faith of Joseph and keep persevering under trial. "So do not throw away your confidence; it will be richly rewarded. You need to persevere so that when you have done the will of God, you will receive what He has promised" (Hebrews 10:35-36).

We may not yet be able to see past the struggle as Joseph did when naming his sons.

I want you to think of one or more of the struggles you are dealing with right now and simply write these four words below in your own handwriting…I trust You, Lord.

I trust You, Lord.

Then I want you to ponder Hebrews 11:1, "Now faith is confidence in what we hope for and assurance about what we do not see." We don't have to know the outcome of how the Lord is going to bring about His perfect will in our lives, we just have to have the confidence in Him that He can and will do it. Just because we cannot perceive a way, doesn't mean there isn't one.

"Forget the former things; do not dwell on the past. See, I am doing a new thing! Now it springs up; do you not perceive it? I am making a way in the wilderness and streams in the wasteland…" Isaiah 43:18-19

Just like Joseph, one day we will forget all our trouble and no longer dwell on the past. I know we can probably already look back at all the ways the Lord has delivered us throughout our lives and He is not finished! His faithfulness remains and He will continue to deliver us, making yet another "way in the wilderness and streams in the wasteland."

Just like Joseph, one day we will forget all our trouble and no longer dwell on the past.

The One who calls you is faithful, and He will do it. 1 Thessalonians 5:24

Day Three: You Are Spies!

For the next seven years, after his glorious deliverance from Potiphar's dungeon, Joseph was busy getting married, having children, and thriving in his new profession as governor over all of Egypt! Those were not only seven years of abundance of food in the land of Egypt, but also seven years of great abundance in Joseph's life! And he certainly did not lie on a bed of ease for those years, but worked very hard, traveling all throughout Egypt and storing food in the city in great quantities.

How important is preparedness to you?

That might seem like a funny question but I know some of us live our lives overly prepared while others prepare for things right at the last minute. Every situation calls for a different set of preparedness but when we look at the way Joseph prepared for the famine, he showed a fair amount of perseverance and stamina. It's interesting to me also that never once do we read of Pharaoh questioning his dreams or his decision to appoint Joseph second–in–command in order to prepare his people for what was to come. As Christians, we know, according to the book of Revelation and really all throughout Scripture that Jesus Christ will return one day.

How can we prepare ourselves and others, especially those who do not know Christ, for His Second Coming?

For it will come on all those who live on the face of the whole earth. Be always on the watch, and pray that you may be able to escape all that is about to happen, and that you may be able to stand before the Son of Man." Luke 21:35-38

What does Luke 21:35-38 say we ought to be doing?

We are all called to live our daily lives working either inside or outside the home, or both, plus doing a million other things to keep life functioning, especially for those are depend on us. However, and I am just as guilty of this, we tend to put all those things first and meet very immediate needs without meeting eternal ones. Or maybe we think that we have got to be doing something ultra–spiritual in order to make an eternal impact. Often the thought of how we cannot attain our lofty ideals actually keeps us from doing the very thing that will make the most difference in God's Kingdom, which is pray. Luke adds in the verb, "watch."

What do you think he means by that?

He could mean that we need to be wise, careful and cautious of the things going on around us. It seems like he is saying, "don't be ignorant of the spiritual condition of your generation, but instead, be alert and pray specifically." We are constantly bombarded by media and social media but sometimes we see the things taking place around us almost like watching a movie instead of remembering it's real life and needs real prayer. I don't expect us to watch FOX news and then pray for every headline news story that we hear, but I do think we can allow the Holy Spirit to impress heavy world issues on our hearts and then pray accordingly. And not just on the worldview spectrum but being alert in our homes, communities, and churches. Sometimes we are too busy to see the spiritual condition of those living right under our roofs. Maybe we need to watch and pray more carefully in order to prepare those we love for things to come. We don't want to try to prepare with few resources in times of famine, but rather use times of abundance to invest where needed.

Maybe we need to watch and pray more carefully in order to prepare those we love for things to come.

When Jacob learned that there was food in Egypt, he said to his sons, "Why do you just keep looking at each other? Genesis 42:1

Joseph invested and prepared so that by the time the famine hit, Egypt provided food to sustain many lives, including those living outside of Egypt.

Who went to Egypt seeking food during the famine (Genesis 42:1-5)?

I absolutely love the way God engineers circumstances! There are no coincidences here as we read of Jacob urging his sons to go to Egypt and buy food for the famine. But notice that Jacob did not send Benjamin with them on their trip (42:4). Even after twenty years of Joseph being gone or dead in Jacob's mind, he still wasn't taking any chances losing his youngest son born to his beloved Rachel.

Go ahead and read Genesis 42:6-17.

When the brothers arrived in Egypt, who did they see and how did he respond to them?

"You are spies!" Something no doubt they had accused him of in the past when asked of his father to check on his brothers! I just cannot help but wonder if Joseph, during those twenty years away from home, not seeing his brothers, ever imagined what he would do if he saw them again! Did he ever lie on the cold, damp dungeon floor thinking of how he wished he had never even gone to look for his brothers that fateful day so long ago? Had hatred planted a seed in his heart, waiting to burst through the soil of his flesh when given the chance for revenge? It seemed so! Those seven years he had prepared to feed the people, but had he prepared himself for such a meeting as he encountered the day his brothers came to town! "As soon as Joseph saw his brothers, he recognized them, but he pretended to be a stranger and spoke harshly to them…" (42:7).

Had hatred planted a seed in his heart, waiting to burst through the soil of his flesh when given the chance for revenge?

How do you think you would have responded to the brothers if you were in Joseph's sandals?

I think I would have just cried! Then in between my messy cry sobs, I may have looked at them, blown my cover right away and said, "Why did you do that to me? Do you have any idea what I have been through the last twenty years? If you think you are getting any food, think again!" Joseph probably didn't know what to do when he saw them. He was probably so shocked that all he could do was be harsh and distant. Remember, those ten men standing in front of him all conspired to kill him as a young teenage boy. He wasn't about to trust them now! If anything, they deserved to be imprisoned. And that's exactly what he did…threw them all in prison on the charges of alleged spies. Still, those three days couldn't come close in comparison with the years Joseph spent in prison! Yet just before he threw them in the slammer, he told them they would be tested in order to prove they were not spies.

And this is how you will be tested: As surely as Pharaoh lives, you will not leave this place unless your youngest brother comes here. Genesis 42:15

What was the test (Genesis 42:15)?

I am big into reading people's facial expressions! Just today, I was in the drive thru at Chick–fil–a and I saw two people sitting outside talking. I couldn't hear what they were saying, but just based on their facial expressions alone I could tell it was a heated discussion! Oh, to have seen the look on the brother's faces when Joseph told them the way they would have to prove they were telling the truth! Just think, for the last twenty years, Jacob had grieved the loss of his beloved firstborn of Rachel. The brother's lived with the disappointment and disgust he felt toward them and yet, even in their hardened hearts, there was still a flicker of remorse. There was enough respect residing among them toward the master of their home that they couldn't fathom putting him through another season of heart wrenching grief. And that is exactly what would have happened if he lost Benjamin too. "If harm comes to him on the journey you are taking, you will bring my gray head down to the grave in sorrow" (42:38b).

Jus t think, for the last twenty years, Jacob you know had grieved the loss of his beloved firstborn of Rachel.

On the third day, Joseph said to them, "Do this and you will live, for I fear God: If you are honest men, let one of your brothers stay here in prison, while the rest of you go and take grain back for your starving households. But you must bring your youngest brother to me, so that your words may be verified and that you may not die." This they proceeded to do. Genesis 42:18-20

Three days in prison possibly softened them to the idea that maybe they should obey this Egyptian governor and bring back Benjamin. I do wonder if they ever stopped to think how strange it was that all this was happening to them.

What was their apparent answer to why they were being questioned and accused upon their arrival in Egypt (Genesis 42:21-22)?

"Didn't I tell you not to sin against the boy? But you wouldn't listen! ...Genesis 42:22

I like how Reuben pipes up and says, "Didn't I tell you not to sin against the boy? But you wouldn't listen! Now we must give an accounting for his blood" (42:22). He was probably sincere in his response and if anything, it seems like all the brothers had enough of a conscience to realize that there was punishment for sin. Today's culture tries to divert all "sinful" behavior into an alternate lifestyle or personality preference. Talking about sin and there being punishment for it is not popular today, even in churches, which is the one place it should be talked about! It's much easier and more seeker–friendly to coddle sin rather than deal with it, confess it, and be cleansed from it. I really feel like so many people who believe they are saved have never, ever, truly and genuinely repented of sin, turned away from it, and sought healing and forgiveness through Christ. That's the very first step to living the Christian life...the very first! No matter how long we have been around churches or in our cultural Christianity circles, we can still live completely defeated lives, in the dark, unless the message of the Cross guides everything we do. The message of the Cross is just that...sin atoned for and forgiven, if we accept fully and wholeheartedly. We should never just visit the Cross, pray to receive Jesus, and then never feel as though living with a spirit of repentance is necessary after that. A motto that I live by is that if I am not feeling the conviction of the Holy Spirit on a regular basis, then I am not growing as a mature follower of Jesus.

Today's culture tries to divert all "sinful" behavior into an alternative lifestyle or personality preference.

According to 1 Thessalonians 4:3-8, what is God's will and His calling for us as Christians (4:3,7)?

The impurity, especially sexual immorality, is staggeringly rampant among our churches today and those who claim to be followers of Christ.

The impurity, especially sexual immorality, is staggeringly rampant among our churches today and those who claim to be followers of Christ. Sadly, they refuse to use the Bible as their standard and make up a religion of their own which eliminates the need for holy living. But it is God's will that we be "sanctified" or as the Amplified Bible puts it, "separated and set apart for pure and holy living." And the calling of God is for us to "live a holy life," or again according to the Amplified, "to dedicate ourselves to the most thorough purity" (4:3,7, Amplified Bible). But none of this can even begin until sin is recognized and revealed in our hearts.

Joseph's brothers recognized their sin and came to the conclusion, just as Paul did in 1 Thessalonians 4:6, that "...no one should wrong his brother or take advantage of him." They were guilty and they knew it, lived with it, and deadened themselves to it, until now. And as they argued over past mistakes, Joseph listened intently.

How did Joseph respond to what the brothers were saying about the day they deserted him (Genesis 42:23-24)?

Can you fathom the emotion! Put yourself in his sandals once again and imagine how the deep pain of the past was resurfacing! It was like an old injury revisiting one's body during a storm. Yet this was no mere injury, it was the pain of his heart, the ache of his body, mind and soul, mixed in a whirlwind of emotional stress and anxiety. And how vulnerable he must have felt, reliving the dark past that had haunted him as he listened to the very men that caused it all to take place! There he was a grown man, thirty years of age, surrounded by men likely in their fifties, and coming to terms with the reality that the Lord had foretold the day when he would see his brothers again in his dreams as a young man. Here's where we just might have an inside look at what the Lord was doing in Joseph's heart. "Although Joseph recognized his brothers, they did not recognize him. Then he remembered his dreams about them…" (Genesis 42:9a). He was beginning to understand God's full plan during the reunion with his brothers, but the first stages of this coming together was no doubt fogged over with grief, anger, sadness, and confusion. Not to mention the sheer fact of wondering if his brothers could even be trusted at all. We cannot say that Joseph's response to them was right or that it was exactly what the Lord wanted him to do. We don't know. But my heart is touched by how the Lord was with Joseph and was softening him, day by day as he saw his brothers and listened to their pleas. Joseph was compassionate and we saw that characteristic of Christ in him from the beginning. At one time he loved his brothers. He cared for them, went looking for them. I don't think he ever wanted to punish them, but the pain of seeing them put his heart through the ringer!

Put yourself in his sandals once again and imagine how the deep the pain of the past was resurfacing!

At one time he loved his brothers. He cared for them, went looking for them. I don't think he ever wanted to punish them, but the pain of seeing them put his heart through the ringer!

He had Simeon taken from them and bound before their eyes. Joseph gave orders to fill their bags with grain, to put each man's silver back in his sack, and to give them provisions for their journey. After this was done for them, they loaded their grain on their donkeys and left. At the place where they stopped for the night one of them opened his sack to get feed for his donkey, and he saw silver in the mouth of his sack. "My silver had been returned," he said to his brothers. "Here it is in my sack." Their hearts sank and they turned to each other trembling and said, "What is this that God has done to us?" Genesis 42:25-28

Simeon, quite possibly the ring leader when it came to how the brothers dealt with Joseph in the past, was bound before their eyes. The Lord could have been using Joseph to give Simeon some extra time to repent and consider his past life of violence. For the guilty perpetrator, the isolation of four prison walls can often aid in some long awaited and much needed self–reflection. Thus the rest of the brothers were sent back home, only to be met with a startling realization upon opening their sacks. Their response, "What is this that God has done to us?" (42:28). Meyer draws truly a heart rending parallel as we consider the spiritual condition of those of us, like the brothers, who fear God as though He were a stranger to whom we cannot relate.

A guilty conscience misinterprets the kindest gifts of mercies which God sends to us, and with evil ingenuity distills poison out of the sweetest flowers. –Meyer

> All this was meant in tender love, but their hearts failed them with fear as they emptied their sacks and saw bundles of money fall out among the grain. A guilty conscience misinterprets the kindest gifts of mercies which God sends to us, and with evil ingenuity distills poison out of the sweetest flowers. How often, like these men, we cry, "What has God done to us?" and are filled with fear when, in point of fact, God's dealings with us brim with blessing and are working out a purpose of mercy which shall make us rejoice all our days.[48]

[48] Meyer, F.B. *Joseph, Beloved, Hated, Exalted.* pg.74-75, CLC Publications: Fort Washington, PA, 2013, ebook.

We can be so shortsighted when faced even with the slightest affliction! We can focus on a tiny dark cloud above luscious ocean beaches and miss the hours of sunlight still left to be enjoyed on the shores of paradise. We can look for a ghost in every closest and lose countless hours of much needed rest. Oh Lord, cleanse us from a guilty conscience so that we can see your mercies all around us, given to us fresh and new every morning! Joseph had freely given his brothers the grain, requiring no payment in return and even gave them enough provisions for their journey so they wouldn't have to eat what they were taking home to their families. Oh sister, the Lord doesn't need us to pay Him back for all that He freely gives to us. He lavishes His blessings on us when we do not deserve them! He purchased us, our souls, through His sacrifice on the Cross. We can never repay Him for that! Nor can we repay Him for His provisions that He uses to sustain us, not only spiritually but materially. All He wants in return is for us to love Him, to trust Him, to live for Him and honor Him with our lives. He wants us to serve Him out of the abundance of what He has given to us. And He wants us to be willing to let Him use whatever means necessary to make us more like Him. And He does all of this for our own good and for our protection. We are on a journey with Jesus through this life and He has already stored up for us all the supplies to meet our every need with every step we take.

...let us draw near to God with a sincere heart and with the full assurance that faith brings, having our hearts sprinkled to cleanse us from a guilty conscience and having our bodies washed with pure water. Hebrews 10:22

Oh Lord, cleanse us from a guilty conscience so that we can see your mercies all around us, given to us fresh and new every morning!

How abundant are the good things that You have stored up for those who fear You, that you bestow in the sight of all, on those who take refuge in You. Psalm 31:19

Day Four: Home and Back Again

After a long journey home, the brothers arrive, still shaken by their experience with Egypt's governor. And more than that, when they realized their money had been put back into their sacks, they thought for sure they had been set up! They were in no hurry to return to Egypt anytime soon, even with the knowledge that Simeon did not return with them. Jacob was soon to be informed of the disturbing events which took place while they were gone.

Read Genesis 42:29-38. How did Jacob react to their story (42:36)?

They were in no hurry to return to Egypt anytime soon...

I know I've given you a lot of reading here lately but as we tackle the last few chapters of the events in Joseph's life, we just have got to read it, as if reading a novel, and try to put ourselves in the scene so we don't miss any details the Lord wants us to highlight. I confess, when writing Bible studies, I want to touch on every single thing that happened in the narrative but time, space, and attention just doesn't always allow it! Plus we need to be able to simmer and meditated on God's Word, allowing it to penetrate our hearts and change our minds. Therefore, if we get bogged down with too many details from the author (that would be me) then we miss the big picture. Hence, I want you to read over slightly larger portions of Scripture yourself so you are getting the whole story.

You with me? Yes/No?

Perfect! I knew you'd say yes!

So as the brothers recounted their frightening stay in Egypt to their father, he began to take the whole thing personal! "Their father Jacob said to them, 'You have deprived me of my children. Joseph is no more and Simeon is no more, and now you want to take Benjamin. Everything is against me!'" Slightly dramatic, but can we blame him? Jacob had zero faith in his older boys, zero. We read very little about the home front in the twenty years Joseph was gone, but there is one story back in Genesis 38:1-30 about Judah and his run in with a prostitute who actually ended up being his daughter in law, who he impregnated and almost had stoned until he realized he was the father of the child! Yes, strange, indeed. You can go back and read the account if you are not already familiar with it but if anything, it goes to show that these sons, who were now grown men with families of their own, were still not men of integrity. Jacob resolved not to let Benjamin go to Egypt, no way, no how! "My son will not go down there with you; his brother is dead and he is the only one left…" (Genesis 42:38a). Jacob seemed to not be able to even mention Benjamin without thinking of his deceased (or so he still believed) son, Joseph. Yet, the threat of starvation can change a man's mind and actions.

Yet, the threat of starvation can change a man's mind and actions.

What did Jacob ask his sons to do in Genesis 43:1-2?

How did Judah respond to him in 43:3-5?

But Judah said to him, "The man warned us solemnly, 'You will not see my face again unless your brother is with you.' Genesis 43:3

These men of Israel were not going back unless they could give Joseph (even though they did didn't know it was him) what he wanted, which was Benjamin. I like how Israel asked, "Why did you bring this trouble on me by telling the man you had another brother" (43:6)? I would have wondered the exact same thing! Oh, and another detail we must mention is that the Lord changed Jacob's name to Israel back in Genesis 32:28, when Jacob wrestled with God. However, Scripture still refers to him as Jacob, instead of Israel all the way up to here in Genesis 43:6! So interesting! He is referred to from this point on as both Jacob and Israel throughout the Bible. I really don't think there is a specific reason for this except that things are about to change for Jacob. Maybe the writer of Genesis wants to remind us that it's not only he, Jacob, that is sending Benjamin, but rather a sign that all of Israel will end up in Egypt. Not a scholar, so not positive about that but found it to be an interesting distinction in this part of the narrative.

They were not only taking Benjamin back to Egypt but also planning on lavishing gifts on this particular Egyptian man who had given them so much trouble!

What were some of those gifts (Genesis 43:11)?

In essence he is saying if I lose him, then I have no more sons left.

Isn't it funny to read about pistachio nuts and almonds in the Bible? If anything, we can definitely relate to the taste of these nuts! But the main thing that Israel emphasized about this second trip wasn't what they were taking back to Egypt but rather a prayer for what they would bring back home. "And may God Almighty grant you mercy before the man so that he will let your other brother and Benjamin come back with you. As for me, I am bereaved, I am bereaved" (43:14). It's still sad to read Jacob saying, "I am bereaved," if he loses Benjamin. In essence he is saying if I lose him, then I have no more sons left. Granted, his other sons acted a mess, but could part of that be due to their father's lack of attention given to them? I approach this with caution only because we don't know how he treated his sons on a daily basis or if they just chose to be rebellious and in turn caused Jacob to turn away from them. But I still think that no matter how he felt toward them, he could have acknowledged more often that they too were his sons, even though born to Leah and the concubines.

What do you think about how Jacob treated his sons after everything we know about their character?

There's really no right or wrong answer here but I was curious as to what you thought about the whole situation. I know we touched on it more at the beginning of our study, especially relating to our own family issues, but it still hurts me to think of siblings being favored over others. In a perfect world, I would hope all parents would treat their children equally, love them equally, but we know that's not the case. And if you are one of other siblings that feel you are not loved as much as you should be, I am sorry. My heart is broken for you. Again, as we discussed earlier in the study, God is no respecter of persons and truly loves us equally as His children. That, my sister is where you find your parental worth and love…in your Heavenly Father. We live in a cursed and broken world, a world that has been offered redemption to those who will accept it through faith in Jesus Christ. We are offered new life, a life that lives above the harsh and cruel circumstances that have imprisoned us emotionally, mentally, and if not at times, physically. Take heart, dear friend, because what you have been given through salvation has the power to uphold your past, present, and future. You no longer have to be bound by relationships that only serve to take advantage of you and leave you feeling abandoned. You may have to go through a process of healing, but you are not alone in that process. The Lord will never abandon you, and if you are willing to keep walking with Him, He will walk you to freedom of your soul, lifting you up into a spacious place and abiding with Him in realms of peace!

You no longer have to be bound by relationships that only served to take advantage of you and leave you feeling abandoned.

Are you in need right now of being lifted up out of the bondage of your circumstances and brought into a spacious place of peace? If so, ask the Lord to help you to persevere until He brings you there.

Joseph may have been taken out of his physical captivity and bondage, but the Lord was still working to free him from the bondage of bitterness toward his brothers.

Read Genesis 43:15-25. Where were the brothers taken upon arrival to Egypt the second time? How did they respond when taken there?

We can imagine that upon entering into Egypt the second time, Joseph's brothers were downright terrified! They really had no idea what to expect after being wrongly accused and watched helplessly as Joseph had Simeon thrown in prison. Therefore, every encounter upon entering into the city was flooded by constant waves of skepticism on their part.

Now the men were frightened when they were taken to his house. They thought, "We were brought here because of the silver that was put back into our sacks the first time. He wants to attack us and overpower us and seize us as slaves and take our donkeys." Genesis 43:18

I am genuinely sad that Joseph's brothers lived their lives up to this point apart from the God of their fathers, never really being able to function without fear and guilt. Not to mention their anger, bitterness, and jealousy which they allowed to rule over themselves for so much of their adult lives. And it would be easy to point the finger at them, shake it back and forth, saying, "shame, shame," but that wouldn't be fair to them or to us. So let's focus for a minute on fear.

Have you ever let fear rule over you, clouding your judgment and making it hard to trust the Lord?

If you are like me at all, before your pen hit the paper, you may have said in your mind, "Umm… yeah!" Fear is one of those terrible weapons the enemy uses to try and stop us from walking in faith, following God's will for our lives. It's kind of like a tasor gun that the enemy shoots at us to stop us dead in our tracks when we are getting close to seeing the Lord work powerfully in our lives. However, when we feel the shock waves of fear surging through our mind, heart, or even tense muscles, we must stand firm in our faith. The kind of faith that says no matter what, I know God is for me and He is powerful enough to continue the work He has started, no matter what things may look like in between. I can honestly say that fear of the future and of failure has plagued me time after time in my life. I hate it. Recently, I just got tired of getting hit with Satan's tasor of fear and choose not to let it affect me. When I feel the waves start to come I speak this simple truth, "Lord, I have surrendered to Your plan whatever that is, so it really doesn't matter what is out there in the future. The future belongs to You and so do I, so I chose to trust You. You are my past, present, and future. Apart from You I have nothing." Listen, Ladies, our goal for the future ought to be Jesus Himself, knowing Him, believing Him, loving Him. So the next time you are hit with the taser of fear, quell the surge with the truth of who God is…capable, powerful, all-knowing, merciful, sovereign, loving, intimate, compassionate, and just over the top wonderful! Then ask yourself, can a God like that ever let me down? No, He can't and He won't! Even when every circumstance begs to deny the very character of Christ, the truth remains, He is the great I AM!

The kind of faith that says no matter what, I know God is for me and He is powerful enough to continue the work He has started, no matter what things may look like in between.

Even when every circumstance begs to deny the very character of Christ, the truth remains, He is the great I AM!

He is the image of the invisible God, the firstborn over all creation. For by Him all things were created: things in heaven and on earth, visible and invisible, whether thrones or powers or rulers or authorities; all things were created by Him and for Him. He is before all things, and in Him all things hold together. Colossians 1:15-17

May God, who puts all things together makes all things whole, Who made a lasting mark through the sacrifice of Jesus, the sacrifice of blood that sealed the eternal covenant, Who led Jesus, our Great Shepherd up and alive from the dead, Now put you together, provide you with everything you need to please Him. Make us into what gives Him most pleasure by means of the sacrifice of Jesus, the Messiah. All glory to Jesus forever and always! Oh, yes, yes, yes. Hebrews 13:20-21, Message

Oh yes, yes, yes! That right there is AWESOME! Saturate your soul in the truth of the supremacy of Jesus Christ and then ask yourself, is there anything that I should be afraid of in light of such power! Whew…I needed that reminder today from Colossians and Hebrews! If it's the future that we are afraid of, we must remember that He will hold it all together, including us, because that's just what He does! And let me tell you, He does it well since He's had a whole lot of experience! I love Him so much I could just get up and dance around my kitchen right now! And if I wasn't afraid of waking the girls, I'd be doing some holy woohooing at a high volume!

If it's the future we are afraid of, we must remember that He will hold it all together, including us, because that's just what He does!

Have I told you lately that I love studying with you! Well, I do! And even though we are wading through the pages of the Old Testament, they feel just as alive and relevant as the latest news story we'd read online today! Tomorrow we will continue to look at the rest of Genesis 43 as we end our fourth week of homework. Can you believe it, you and I have already spent nineteen days studying Joseph together! I'm so proud of you and I pray that the Lord has embedded some serious truths from His Word over these last four weeks deep within the bedrock of your heart. I know He has mine! Love you!

Day Five: Abundant Proportion

Have you ever gotten upset with your spouse, a friend, or other close family member and even though you forgave them for what they did, you still brought up their past offense in fits of anger or frustration? My husband says I remember things he has done in the past that upset or hurt me because I have a strong emotion attached to them. Sometimes when I'm upset with him, instead of keeping to the immediate issue at hand, I'll bring up something hurtful he did in the past. For example, when we are arguing about how he forgot to bring me flowers for my birthday (I love getting flowers!) I'll often regrettably say, "You didn't remember them last year either!" Then I find myself upset about not getting flowers for two birthdays instead of just one! See what I mean?

My husband says I remember things he has done in the past that upset or hurt me because I have a strong emotion attached to them.

Can you think of a time when you forgave once but in light of another hurtful offense, brought the past hurt back up again, finding yourself doubly upset?

Now there are allowances for trying to show someone there is a pattern of a repeated problem, like repeatedly forgetting flowers every year after eleven years of marriage (I'm not bitter or anything!) Ha-ha! But the main thing I am trying to help us understand is what Joseph may have been experiencing in his dealings with his brothers. Everything he did was fueled by a flood of emotions from the past of offenses done to him by his brothers. Today we will see the pendulum swing for the young (to me thirties is young!) governor of Egypt once again as he plays nice then not so nice!

Going back to yesterday's chapter, go ahead and read Genesis 43:26-34.

In what ways did Joseph play nice during this particular encounter with his brothers?

A very pleasant Joseph emerged from behind the drawn curtains, accepting gifts, asking about the men's aged father and clarifying if the young man with them was indeed their younger brother, Benjamin (43:26-29).

How did Joseph respond after seeing Benjamin (43:29-30)?

Honestly, I am amazed that Joseph kept his identity hidden as long as he did!

Doesn't his response just move you to tears! Honestly, I am amazed that Joseph kept his identity hidden as long as he did! If it were me, I would have blown my cover long before now. When he saw Benjamin, the Amplified Bible says, "And Joseph hurried from the room, for his heart yearned for his brother, and he sought privacy to weep; so he entered his chamber and wept there" (43:30). I can imagine that in the mix of the emotional upheaval, Joseph yearned for the years with Benjamin that were lost by their separation. Notice that when Joseph saw his other brothers, anger welled up inside of him. But upon seeing Benjamin, he remembered not the dreadful day he was thrown into the pit, but rather the years proceeding. Surely he recounted the years with his beloved father and mother and playing with his younger brother on carefree days, running throughout the foothills of Northwest Mesopotamia and Canaan. The memories of the last thirty plus years of his life surged through him like floodwaters with no boundaries and he could no longer contain his overwhelming emotion. In an effort to fully release his grief, he raced to his personal chambers and cried off all of his Egyptian makeup.

Do you remember a time in your life when you were reunited with a family member or friend and you could not contain your overwhelming emotion at the sight of them?

Surely he recounted the years with his beloved father and mother and playing with his younger brother on carefree days, running throughout the foothills of Northwest Mesopotamia and Canaan.

I am such a cry baby! I'll cry at the drop of a hat...but bring back a long lost friend or tell me I have to say goodbye to someone I love and I turn to mush. I've watched reunions of military men and women coming home from overseas and even though I don't know them, seeing their emotion almost always makes me cry my face off! Benjamin may as well have been coming home from Afghanistan back to Egypt to see his older brother since the scene was just as dramatic! It's safe to say, Joseph cried his face right off!

After he had washed his face, he came out and, controlling himself, said, "Serve the food" (Genesis 43:31).

If we look back at 43:33-34, we will see that Joseph did not sit with his brothers as they ate, nor did any of the Egyptian attendants in the household. Scripture says, "...Egyptians could not eat with Hebrews, for that is detestable to Egyptians" (43:32b). James G. Murphy, in his Barnes Notes, says, "They [they Egyptians] considered all foreigners unclean, and therefore refused to eat with them."[49] According to Herodotus's ancient writings, one reason for the Egyptians particularly not wanting to eat with the Israelites was that they did not eat the meat of female cows, whereas the Israelites ate both male and female. Male cows, if clean, were acceptable to eat by Egyptians, however, the females were not to be eaten since they were sacred to Isis, one of the Egyptian female

[49] Murphy, James G. *Barnes Notes*, pg 476-477, Baker Book House: Grand Rapids, MI, 1987.

goddesses.[50] Since Joseph wasn't allowed to eat with his brothers, what he did next absolutely astonished them all the more!

What was the seating arrangement for the brothers and were there any differences in their food proportions (Gen 43:33-34)?

And [Joseph's brothers] were given seats before him–the eldest according to his birthright and the youngest according to his youth; and the men looked at one another amazed [that so much was known about them]. Genesis 43:33, Amp.

Those Hebrew men around the strange Egyptian's table probably thought they were in the twilight zone! Nevertheless, this was one zone worth partaking in! We can imagine that the brothers probably had not had meat or any sort of extravagant food in quite some time due to the famine. So they wasted no time in feasting and drinking freely with Joseph (43:34). Even though they were at different tables, there was still the sense of ease and acceptance among the brothers, especially with Benjamin! He was given quite a large portion compared to the rest of the brothers. Evidently, Joseph was making an extra effort to show Benjamin that he had not requested his presence in Egypt to reprimand him, but rather, reward him! I cannot help but draw a beautiful parallel to the way Christ deals with us when we draw near to Him. So often we are afraid to approach Him in fear that He will be upset with us or disappointed. But nothing could be further from the truth! He desires for us to be in His presence constantly. Christ gave His life so we could live twenty–four seven in the presence of a Holy God! Hebrews 4:14-16 reminds us just how much Christ can sympathize with what it's like to live in this sin trodden flesh!

For we do not have a high priest who is unable to sympathize with our weaknesses...Hebrews 4:15a

Therefore, since we have a great high priest who has gone through the heavens, Jesus the Son of God, let us hold firmly to the faith we profess. For we do not have a high priest who is unable to sympathize with our weaknesses, but we have One who has been tempted in every way, just as we are–yet was without sin. Let us then approach the throne of grace with confidence, so that we may receive mercy and find grace to help us in our time of need (Hebrews 4:14-16).

I want you to underline the truths in those verses that speak out to you today. I know for me, knowing that Jesus can understand what I am going through and how weak and prone to falling into temptation I am just makes me want to be near Him all the more! Listen, my sister, if you feel like no one in this world really "gets" you or understands you, you can trust that Your Father in Heaven does! He not only gets you, He made you and knows exactly what you need, even when you don't! So please don't ever feel like He is unapproachable. Now, before I get myself in a fix, Paul does tell us in 1 Timothy 6:16 that our God, "dwells in unapproachable light," but He is speaking of His all–surpassing glory! Now, if we want to visibly see that glory, we have either got to have a major heavenly vision from God, or be dead! But the approachability I am speaking of and Hebrews speaks of, is on a day to day, spiritual, relational level. Through our prayers, we can approach God's throne, knowing that if we humbly, obediently come to Him, confessing our sin (daily sins), He hears us! And He is there, willing and able to do abundantly, immeasurably more than we could ever ask or imagine (Ephesians 3:20)!

He not only gets you, He made you and knows exactly what you need, even when you don't!

Joseph gave his younger brother of the same mother, Benjamin, an abundant proportion of food showing him favor in the sight of his older brothers. Oh, if we could only understand how much favor we have been shown simply because of our position in the Heavenly family as the children of God!

---

[50] Murphy, James G. *Barnes Notes*, pg 476-477, Baker Book House: Grand Rapids, MI, 1987.

See what great love the Father has lavished on us, that we should be called children of God! And that is what we are (1 John 3:1a)!

That is what we are! We are children of a God who gave His Son, His only Son, to die a sinners' death in order for us to receive the same inheritance as Jesus. And that inheritance is eternal life and all the spiritual blessings that one could ever dream of asking for in this life and the one to come! What spiritual blessings in this life, you may ask? Well, how about victory over sin, possessing an abundance of spiritual fruit (love, joy, peace, patience, gentleness…), and being a living witness for Christ. Being a witness for Christ means seeing the Lord work not only in our lives, but in the lives of others around us and participating with Him in that work!

Being a witness for Christ means seeing the Lord work not only in our lives, but in the lives of others around us and participating with Him in that work!

What are some other spiritual blessings that come to your mind?

We are blessed beyond measure to hold the very Word of God in our hands, which contains hundreds of promises given to us as spiritual blessings in Christ Jesus. "For no matter how many promises God has made, they are "Yes" in Christ. And so through Him the "Amen" is spoken by us to the glory of God" (2 Cor 1:20). Believing and placing our faith in Christ is the key that unlocks all the promises made to us in God's Word. When we ask God to fulfill in our lives what He has already spoken in His Word, we can know that when we say "Amen," God will gain the glory even before the answer is received! Our job is not to try and guess exactly how He is going to bring about the outcome to the circumstances in our lives, but rather that He will do it exactly according to His will in order to gain glory for Himself. If we want to bring God glory, we must trust His will and His ways. We must cling to the promise and leave the rest up to the Lord.

My dear friend, you may be in a situation today wondering, "How in the world is the Lord going to accomplish this major issue in my life?" Let me reassure you that He can and He will. Don't look to the outcome but rather…

… "How in the world is the Lord going to accomplish this major issue in my life?" Let me reassure you that He can and He will.

…[looking away from all that will distract us and] focusing our eyes on Jesus, who is the Author and Perfecter of faith [the first incentive for our belief and the One who brings our faith to maturity], who for the joy [of accomplishing the goal] set before Him endured the cross, disregarding the shame, and sat down at the right hand of the throne of God [revealing His deity, His authority, and the completion of His work] (Hebrews 12:2, Amp).

The Lord may have you in a place where you are enduring suffering in order to see the completed work of Christ in your life. We can't stop and give up along the journey. We must continue onto the destination. Heaven is the ultimate promise and Jesus has made a way for us to finish strong, being sure that He will finish what He has started in us!

LESSON FOUR
The Savior of the World

Parallels in Scripture are surely more than a coincidence. –Meyer[51]

I. Joseph's new name, given him by Pharaoh, was Zaphenath–paneah, which means Savior of the ___________ and Revealer of _________________ (Gen. 41:45).

> *–And we have seen and testify that the Father has sent his Son to be the Savior of the world (1 John 4:14).*
>
> *–The king said to Daniel, "Surely your God is the God of gods and the Lord of kings and a revealer of mysteries, for you were able to reveal this mystery" (Dan. 2:47).*

II. Joseph's wife, Asenath, represents Christ's marriage to the _______________ peoples.

> *–Then Paul and Barnabas answered them boldly: "We had to speak the word of God to you first. Since you reject it and do not consider yourselves worthy of eternal life, we now turn to the Gentiles (Acts 13:46).*
>
> –Joseph was cast out by his ___________ , just as Christ has been rejected by many of the Jews who still do not ______________ Him to be the Messiah.

III. Both the _____________ and the _____________, whom Joseph took pity on represent the two thieves on the cross with Jesus (Luke 23:39-43).

IV. Joseph was exalted to a _____________ of _____________ (Gen. 41:41-43).

> *–He [Pharaoh] had him ride in his second chariot; and they proclaimed before him, "Bow the knee!" And he set him over all the land of Egypt (41:43, NASB).*
>
> *–It is written: "As surely as I live,' says the Lord, 'every knee will bow before Me; every tongue will acknowledge God'" (Romans 14:11).*
>
> *–Therefore God exalted him to the highest place and gave Him the name that is above every name, that at the name of Jesus every knee should bow, in heaven and on earth and under the earth, and every tongue acknowledge that Jesus Christ is Lord, to the glory of God the Father (Phil. 2:9-11).*

V. Joseph provided bread for a ___________ famine. Jesus is the Bread of Life for our _____________ famine!

> *– Then Jesus declared, "I am the bread of life. Whoever comes to Me will never go hungry, and whoever believes in Me will never be thirsty" (John 6:35).*

---

[51] Meyer, F.B. *Joseph, Beloved, Hated, Exalted.* pg. 61-62, CLC Publications: Fort Washington, PA, 2013, Kindle Version.

GROUP DISCUSSION QUESTIONS

The Savior of the World

1. What parallel of Joseph and Jesus from our lesson intrigued you the most?

2. How does the parallel of Joseph's wife and Christ marrying Himself to a pagan, Gentile people help you to understand how we could never earn our salvation? Do you ever feel completely undeserving of Christ's love for you? If so, how does the reminder that "while we were yet sinners, Christ died for us" help you to fully accept His free gift of salvation?

3. What are some of the ways in our generation do we see a spiritual famine taking place?

4. How did the last quote read in our lesson speak to you? Have you transferred your Savior "to some obscure dungeon in your heart," as Meyer suggested? If so, how can you free Him in order to allow Him to rule over every area of your life?

WEEK FIVE:
Reunited and Rested

Day One: A Riveting Reveal

I can hardly believe we are sitting together today to begin day one of our last week of homework! I am so proud of you for working so hard and studying the life of Joseph with me in–depth. Whether or not you are familiar with in–depth Bible studies or if this is your first one, I pray the Lord has worked deeply in your heart and life up to this point in our study. I know He has mine! Scripture NEVER fails to change me every time I wade in the waters of God's living and active Word. It either calls me to surge with conviction and zeal, or it begs me to be still and know how holy and awesome our God is!

What are some of the ways the Lord has spoken directly to you over the last four weeks of our time together? Try to name at least one specific thing if you can!

Scripture NEVER fails to change me every time I wade in the waters of God's living and active Word.

One of the ways the Lord gets us through certain, potentially difficult seasons along life's journey is by causing us to ponder His past faithfulness. Looking back at what He has already spoken to us gives us the strength to continue on in the present and into the future! Is not the Bible a book full of promises spoken long ago…way back in the past? Yet, its power is just as much alive to us today as it was thousands of years ago! Joseph's life, lived from roughly 1915AD to 1805AD is still being used by God to sow deep spiritual truths into our lives. I would never consider myself a historian, but Biblical history is something I can definitely get into! There's a payoff when it comes to immersing yourself into the past with the Ancient of Days Himself!

Speaking of being immersed, as we begin our lesson today, we will see how Joseph was still engrossed with his brothers' most recent visit to Egypt and his continued resistance to reveal his true identity to them.

There's a payoff when it comes to immersing yourself in the past with the Ancient of Days Himself!

Go ahead and read Genesis 44:1-34.

Why do you think Joseph had his silver cup placed in Benjamin's sack rather than letting all the brothers go back home together? There is really no right or wrong answer here, I'm just wondering your thoughts after reading the chapter.

Time really does not allow us to dissect all of chapter 44 as much as I would really like to. However, there are a few things that we can highlight prior to jumping into chapter 45. First of all, we can see that Joseph was not willing to part with Benjamin so soon after their lavish dinner together! Nor was Joseph ready to reveal his identity to them quite yet, therefore he devised another cheeky plan to get them all to come back to Egypt.

How was Joseph's steward to describe the silver cup to his brothers in Genesis 44:5?

Divination, by definition according to Wycliffe is, "the attempt to discern future events by such means as trances, visions, etc., or physical objects."[52] Therefore when we read in verse 5 that the silver cup Joseph drank out of was used for divination, it could be a reference to the way most pagan governors and Pharaohs also used their cups. However, we mustn't let this confuse us about Joseph's integrity. He allowed God Himself to tell of future events, as He had done in the interpretation of all the dreams previously.

> In order to confuse his brethren, Joseph had his servants suggest the goblet found in their sacks for that purpose (Gen 44:5, 15); no approval of such a practice is implied. God sternly condemns all means of seeking hidden knowledge and knowledge of the future apart from His divine revelation.[53]

I have to guard my heart and take my burdens to the Lord.

Joseph continued to go to the extreme by further hiding his identity, even lying about using divination. According to what we have already read, it seems the brothers were already terrified upon seeing a silver cup in Benjamin's sack. Regardless of what it was used for, it meant that they could not continue their journey back home to their father Jacob. Like Joseph, I confess I can take things to the extreme. I have to guard my heart and take my burdens to the Lord. If not, I can take a mole hill and turn it into a mountain really fast in my overanxious thought process.

When I try to control things, I eventually end up panicking big time.

What about you? Are you an extremist? What are some ways you can combat turning a mole hill into a mountain?

I know for me, I've got to get into God's Word, pray, and simply not let myself take things to the next level of anxiety. I've also got to leave the future up to the Lord since He's the only One that can handle it, not me! When I try to control things, I eventually end up panicking big time. Joseph had a similar panicked reaction after he realized that this time he'd gone a little too far with the silver cup.

In a moment of clarity, Joseph realized the last person on earth he wanted to harm was his dear, beloved father.

Who did Joseph not realize he was hurting by wanting to retain his brother Benjamin (Gen 44:30-32)?

In a moment of clarity, Joseph realized that the last person on earth he wanted to harm was his dear, beloved father. In a sudden rush of emotion, his game of hidden identity came to a screeching halt!

Then Joseph could no longer control himself before all his attendants, and he cried out, "Have everyone leave my presence!" So there was no one with Joseph when he made himself known to his brothers. And he wept so loudly that the Egyptians heard him, and Pharaoh's household heard about it. Joseph said to his brother, "I am Joseph! Is my father living?" But his brothers were not able to answer him, because they were terrified at his presence (Genesis 45:1-3).

---

[52] Pfeiffer, Charles F., Vos, Howard F., Rea, John, *Wycliffe Bible Dictionary.* pg. 468, "Divination." Hendrickson Publishers, Inc: Mass, 2001.
[53] Ibid.

What a long awaited moment! Finally Joseph could fully give himself to his brothers without holding anything back. The series of tests he had put them through was over and the veil was now removed. His true feelings, his unwavering love, despite the harsh treatment he had endured from the men standing before him, triumphed by the gift of grace he was extending. Truly Joseph possessed the heart of God! A beautiful analogy of the Father's unconditional love given to us is summed up in the *Messages of the Morning Watch.*

What a long awaited moment! Finally Joseph could fully give himself to his brothers without holding anything back.

> So it is always: *real sacrifice, unto complete surrender of self, brings to us the revelation of God in His fullness.* As we have already seen, it was only on condition of Jacob's releasing and the brothers' bringing the best they had, Benjamin, that they could even see Joseph's face again. And when Judah went farther than this, offered himself to be Joseph's slave forever, then it was that Joseph could keep back nothing, but found himself compelled to reveal everything to those for whom his heart yearned. It is God's own way with us. God in Jesus Christ does not, and apparently cannot, make Himself fully known in His personality and love, until we have surrendered to Him unconditionally and forever not only all we have but all we are. *Then God can refrain no longer, but lavishes upon us, in Christ, such a revealing of Himself that it cannot be told in words.*[54]

So is it always: real sacrifice, unto complete surrender of self, brings to us the revelation of God in His fullness.

Unless we give ourselves fully to the Lord, holding nothing back, we will never fully understand the gift of grace and forgiveness extended to us in Jesus Christ. Jacob (Joseph's father) surrendered Benjamin to be taken to Egypt, having to trust that the Lord would protect him. Judah, another one of Joseph's brothers, surrendered himself to be Joseph's slave before Joseph revealed his true identity. Therefore, as the *Messages of the Morning Watch* relate the surrender of the brothers to our own need for surrender, we come to understand that "real sacrifice, unto complete surrender of self, brings to us the revelation of God in His fullness." I cannot even begin to fully describe the accuracy of this truth as it played out in my own life! I grew up knowing Christ and having been taught the Bible, nearly in its entirety. Yet the older I became, the more I found myself separated from the Lord due to my lack of obedience and desire not to live according to His Word. I thought I loved Him, I thought I knew Him, but I merely was fond of Him and knew OF Him. I withheld from yielding myself to the Holy Spirit's conviction. I lived my life as I chose and then paid lip service to all I had been taught. Therefore, the Lord was under no obligation to reveal Himself to me since I was in no state to see Him for who He truly is. Finally, in my early twenties, I began to surrender myself fully to Him, to throw myself at His feet in desperation for His mercy to change me and to rescue me from the death grip of sin and rebellion. That's the surrender He was waiting for! Oh my sister, since then, my life has been so dramatically different.

Therefore, the Lord was under no obligation to reveal Himself to me since I was in no state to see Him for who He truly is.

What about you? Have you fully surrendered to your Savior? I mean real surrender, like giving Him everything you are and everything you have. Beloved, unless you let Him have it all, you will never really know Him.

[54] Cowman, Charles E. Mrs., *Springs in the Valley.* pg. 34-35. Zondervan Publishing House: Grand Rapids MI., 1997, Kindle Version.

Seeing how startled and distressingly disturbed his brothers were, how did Joseph console them after revealing his identity (Genesis 45:4-8)?

Oh, if we could only look back over our lives as Joseph did and see that the hand of an all–knowing God was guiding us all the way for a glory greater than we could ever imagine!

What a glorious perspective! Oh, if we could only look back over our lives as Joseph did and see that the hand of an all–knowing God was guiding us all the way for a glory greater than we could ever imagine! Finally in the presence of a brother who they thought dead, they received forgiveness and acceptance. And all because Joseph understood that the school of suffering he experienced was really a school of training in order to be used by God in the saving of many lives. Sadly, we live in a culture that is so self–centered and self–serving that we cannot fathom submitting our lives wholly to God in order for Him to use us mightily in the lives of others. We get so focused on God's plan for us and lose sight of God's plan to use us to minister to others. And in order to equip us for such a task, we may have to experience some hardships so that we can relate to what those around us are experiencing. So instead of saying, what's in it for me, we should be praying, "God use me and whatever You need to allow in order for me to be effective for Your service, so be it!" Oh goodness, easier prayed than done, especially when the heat of affliction is turned up in our lives. But if we trust the Lord to carry out the work He has started in us, we can be sure He will complete it!

We get so focused on God's plan for us and lose sight of God's plan to use us to minister to others.

When we see Joseph extending grace and forgiveness to his brothers, we see a life that has come full circle and the heart of a man who looks to the Lord as the great Shepherd of his life. As he looks upon his brothers with compassion, he says, "So then, it was not you who sent me here, but God. He made me father to Pharaoh, lord of his entire household and ruler of all Egypt" (Genesis 45:8). It was not you…but God! How easy to have blamed his brothers for everything he endured in his past! How easy for us to point the finger at somebody, anybody, or anything and allow bitterness to grow up inside of us and choke the life out of us. How different, how free would we feel if we could say with confidence…"but God!" We have the opportunity today to be free if we choose to take it. What has held you in the grip of bitterness and resentment? Who or what are you still blaming deep down inside?

Accepting His plan for our lives, even if it looks nothing like we expected, will free us from living enslaved to our past.

I want you to fill in the blank. "It was not ______________________________ that brought me to this place, but God."

Accepting His plan for our lives, even if it looks nothing like we expected, will free us from living enslaved to our past. However, one aspect of this we must consider is that unlike Joseph, if we have a past full of sinful behavior, consequences of that sin may have been the cause for some of our pain. I know God did not bring me into a place of willful sinful behavior when I was a teenager. Yet even after a long season of rebellion, I was still extended mercy and grace after repenting and surrendering my life to Christ, choosing to walk in obedience to Him. Nevertheless, over the last decade, even after walking in obedience to the Lord, I have experienced hardships that I never would have chosen for myself or my family to experience. It has been after those seasons that I learned to accept those sufferings from God's hand, knowing He will use them for His glory. As a matter of fact, I think it's safe to say, quite possibly in both your life and mine, He already has!

For our light and momentary troubles are achieving for us an eternal glory that far outweighs them all. So we fix our eyes not on what is seen, but on what is unseen. For what is seen is temporary, but what is unseen is eternal (2 Corinthians 4:17-18).

Day Two: A Joyous Journey

Joseph came to a place in his life where God mercifully, after many years of heartache, firmly planted those he loved.

I cannot think of a more wonderful feeling than knowing my family is safe and sound. Whether it be immediate family or even distant, when we know everyone is being well taken care of, our minds are at ease. Many a mother worries about the welfare of her children, siblings, aging parents, close friends, and so on. But when we know all is well, we are well. If only that were always the case! Joseph came to a place in his life where God mercifully, after many years of heartache, firmly planted those he loved. After the emotional upheaval of his brother's reunion, there was a refreshing calm that washed over Egypt's governor and awakened his desire to be a shepherd for his people, Israel. He embraced his brothers, wept over them and then enjoyed a bittersweet reunion. Word got around very quickly that Egypt's governor had been reunited with his brothers! "When the news reached Pharaoh's palace that Joseph's brothers had come, Pharaoh and all his officials were pleased" (Genesis 45:16). Pharaoh wasted no time in sending his approval of all that had transpired.

What did Pharaoh direct Joseph's family to do and what did he promise them (Genesis 45:17-23)?

Joseph reminded his brothers not to do what on their journey home (45:24)?

We would be crazy not to see the clear and unfathomable parallel to how our Savior deals with us!

Talk about winning the Egyptian lottery! And just when the brothers thought the day could not get any more bizarre after seeing their brother, basically back from the dead in their minds, now to have received the overwhelming favor of Pharaoh himself! You know they had to be thinking in their minds, "We do not deserve this! We deserve death for what we did to you Joseph! And here you are forgiving us, pardoning our sin against you and then showering us with all these possessions, not to mention giving us a new homeland to settle in?" I can imagine that it was all too much for these weary men to take in! We would be crazy not to see the clear and unfathomable parallel to how our Savior deals with us. When we come to him, on our knees, crying out in all humility for His forgiveness, He reveals Himself to us, pardons our sin, showers us with blessings both materially and spiritually, then settles us in His family as one of His own dear, beloved children! If we have experienced this kind of saving grace from our Heavenly Father, then it too may have left us saying, "I don't deserve this! I deserve death for all the sin I have committed in my lifetime! And here You are forgiving me, pardoning my sin and showering me with all these blessings, not to mention giving me an eternal place in Heaven with You as your daughter!"

How does Psalm 103:9-14 and 1 Peter 1:3-5 validate how undeserving we are of the Lord's favor on us?

He does not treat us as our sins deserve or repay us according to our iniquities. Psalm 103:10

Knowing how mercifully God has dealt with us ought to compel us to live for Him! It ought to compel us to persevere when the going gets tough, to passionately seek His face and trust Jesus with everything we are and everything we have. It ought to cause us to weep tears of deep gratitude for a God who sent His one and only Son to take our place, experience death, and rise again so that we too could have an inheritance that will never perish, spoil, or fade. It ought to beg us to live lives of holiness and obedience, desiring to put aside our foolish ways and take hold of the power that we are given by the Holy Spirit of God to overcome temptation. In light of such forgiveness, how can we ignore the response that is demanded of us! Joseph expected the same of his brothers to a certain degree when he told them, "…Don't quarrel on the way [back home]!" (Genesis 45:24, brackets mine). Surely Joseph had remembered many days gone by when the brothers walked and traveled together herding sheep all the while fighting and quarreling with each other. After having said it, quite possibly the brothers looked back at him with a half-hearted smile, knowing that if anyone was familiar with their behavior, it was Joseph.

In light of such forgiveness, how can we ignore the response that is demanded of us!

Their journey back home with the good news of Joseph's appearance not only brought with it a message for Jacob but also a wealth of material possessions! Once again we see great favor shown to Benjamin from Joseph, in some ways the same favor Joseph had been shown as a child by his father. Therefore, it looks like the fault of favoritism carried itself through another generational line. Yet, the brothers, as far as we know, were not about to complain about it this time! "To each of them he gave new clothing, but to Benjamin he gave three hundred shekels of silver and five sets of clothing" (45:22). And of course, Joseph sent lavish gifts to his father to prove that the message he was about to receive was the real thing (45:23).

How did Jacob react when he heard the unbelievable news (Genesis 45:25-28)?

…the spirit of their father Jacob revived. Genesis 45:27

"They told him, 'Joseph is still alive! In fact, he is ruler of all Egypt.' Jacob was stunned; he did not believe them" (Genesis 45:26). I think to say he was stunned is definitely an understatement! The Amplified version gives us a little more to go on in its translation of verse 26.

And they said to him, Joseph is alive! And he is governor over all the land of Egypt! And Jacob's heart began to stop beating and [he almost] fainted, for he did not believe them (Genesis 45:26).

I should say so! It's a wonder he didn't die immediately of shock! But we both know that the Lord would not have let that happen. His divine plan was to gloriously reunite the family, even if it did seem like the eleventh hour. With God, it's never too late. Just when you think one of your greatest hearts desires is dead and gone, the Lord brings it to life right before your very eyes.

Have you experienced an answer to one of your deepest longings or specific prayers after thinking they had been long forgotten?

What about the endless prayers to see a loved one saved and then after years of waiting, they come to know the Lord. Or waiting for the Lord to bring you a spouse and out of nowhere, there he is! Maybe it's the long awaited job, child, return of a child, promotion, marriage restored, or college acceptance? The list could go on and on. Or what if you are in the waiting stage right now, waiting patiently or some days painfully, for the Lord to bring the answer?

But do not forget this one thing, dear friends: With the Lord a day is like a thousand years, and a thousand years is like a day. 2 Peter 3:8

Are you waiting or have been waiting for a long time for the Lord to fulfill your deepest desire or answer a seemingly endless prayer?

Take delight in the Lord, and He will give you the desires of your heart. Psalm 37:4

Remember, my sweet friend, if what you desire or what you are praying for is part of God's plan, He will see it through. It may look different or come later than you would have originally planned, but if it's coming from Him it will certainly come. "...Though it linger, wait for it; it will certainly come and will not delay" (Habakkuk 2:3b). I cannot even tell you how many times I have taken comfort in knowing that the Lord will make good on His promises. However, I must always keep my desires, prayers, and longings open to being changed if they are not in line with His promises or plans for my life. Basically what it comes down to is that if the Lord doesn't want it or have it planned for me, then I don't want it either. There is freedom when we can give Him full control over our lives to do what He pleases. It seems, according to Psalm 37:4 that our job is to delight ourselves in Jesus and He will take care of the rest. And when you think about it, that's not a bad job! Of course it doesn't mean we just sit around and feel delightful. But what is does mean is that we seek to find full satisfaction in our Savior as we live the life He has laid out for us. It also means we live in the present, not in the future. We do not know what a year, a month, a week, a day, an hour, or five minutes will hold. But we can keep our focus on Christ, who is available to us twenty four hours a day, seven days a week. We can go to Him and we can trust Him with our prayers, desires, and our futures.

Basically what it comes down to is that if the Lord doesn't want it or have it planned for me, then I don't want it either.

Jacob had spent many years grieving the loss of his beloved son Joseph and the news of him not only being very much alive but ruler of all Egypt was just too good to be true! Yet, after his spirit was revived, he was convinced that what he heard was indeed the truth! "And Israel said, "I'm convinced! My son Joseph is alive. I will go and see him before I die" (Genesis 45:28). Therefore, with pep in his step, he gathered up the family, seventy in all, and headed for Goshen in Egypt (45:27). His first stop, however, was Beersheba.

What did Jacob do at Beersheba and how did God respond (Genesis 46:1-4)?

What a beautiful confirmation! Don't you know that even though Jacob had heard the astonishing news and gathered up all he had, there still must have been some lingering doubt in his mind. Should he really go up to Egypt and live there, leaving the land promised to both he and his forefathers? And when you are 130 years old, you don't usually just pick up and move! Even Abraham wasn't that old when he moved. Still, Jacob needed to be reassured in his old age that he was doing the right thing, and God did not withhold that reassurance. "I am God, the God of your father. Do not be afraid to go down to Egypt, for I will make you into a great nation there" (46:3). Years before, the Lord had appeared to Jacob in a dream near Beersheba and now He was reminding Jacob, I am still God and I am still going to make good on My promises to you (28:10-15). Oh, how we need that fresh reminder that God is still God and will not abandon us on this journey we call life! When we seek Him, come to Him in all humility and brokenness, He answers us, instructs us, comforts us and reminds us of all His promises made to us. All He asks of us is that we draw near to Him, refrain from turning our backs on Him and diligently seek Him in His Word. Jacob trusted the Lord to guide Him, even on the last leg of his journey. He pressed on, and we must do the same.

...I will not leave you until I have done what I have promised you. Genesis 28:15b

Now Jacob sent Judah ahead of him to Joseph to get directions to Goshen. When they arrived in the region of Goshen, Joseph had his chariot made ready and went to Goshen to meet his father Israel. As soon as Joseph appeared before him, he threw his arms around his father and wept for a long time. Genesis 46:28-29

Oh, how we need that fresh reminder that God is still God and will not abandon us on this journey we call life!

Can you even imagine the anticipation Joseph and Jacob must have felt as they both approached Goshen? It was almost too good to be true! A father and son who thought they'd never see each other again; a father who had been convinced for years that his son was dead. A son who thought that surely his father had already died of old age. But as the hoofs of Joseph's chariot kicked up the dust and wheels of Jacob's donkey cart turned, the approaching silhouettes of what for so many years had only been a mirage in their minds was finally taking shape to become the reunion of a lifetime. Goshen, which means "drawing near," was a region in lower Egypt, east of the Nile, and by its name, clearly it held a significance unlike any other.[55]

Ponder for a moment the sweetness of this father and son reunion as you read Genesis 46:29-30. What touches your heart the most?

So many stories to tell, so many heartaches to heal, so many loving embraces to be shared, but for that moment, no words would suffice.

All I can think of is the word, "relief." There must have been such an immense sigh of relief among the many shed tears knowing for that one moment in time, all was right in the world. So many stories to tell, so many heartaches to heal, so many loving embraces to be shared, but for that moment, no words would suffice. And after their long embrace, Jacob peeled his son away, yet only to arms–length in order to look straight into his eyes and say with confidence, "Now I am ready to die, since I have seen for myself that you are still alive" (46:30). The father of all Israel, who had held onto a thin thread of hope, had finally seen God do what he thought for so many long and painful years could never be done. And yet, after seeing that God had been in control the entire time, was able to say, "I see for myself that the Lord kept you safer than I ever could, my son, and never let you go, not for a moment."

[55] "H1657-Goshen-Strong's Hebrew Lexicon (KJV). "Blue Letter Bible. Web. 5 June 2017. www.blueletterbible.org

Day Three: The Land is Before You

With a spirit revived and a son alive, Jacob and the rest of the family began the journey to their new homeland. The excitement must have been paramount! Joseph, having yearned and longed for many years to go home to his family, had instead brought his family to Egypt! Surely there were new faces among the household since he had last gazed upon the hills of Canaan. Even his baby brother, Benjamin, who was now in his mid–thirties, had ten sons (Genesis 46:21)! Once the dust settled in the fertile land of Goshen, with all his family accounted for, Joseph put his organizing and administering skills to work in order to safely settle them in their new land.

It was no small thing to gain an audience with Pharaoh.

How did Joseph want his brothers and father to respond to Pharaoh upon meeting him (Genesis 46:31-34)?

It was no small thing to gain an audience with Pharaoh. Yet it was not because of the family itself, but rather because of Joseph. Therefore, Joseph carefully chose five of his brothers to accompany him in the presence of Pharaoh. We can almost be certain he chose Benjamin and quite possibly Reuben, maybe even Judah. Yet I would imagine he left Simeon and Levi back at the camp. We can only guess who Joseph took but one thing is sure, he had prepped them all for the kingly encounter with the ruler of Egypt! And sure enough, Pharaoh asked the very question Joseph had already anticipated him asking.

Pharaoh asked the brothers, "What is your occupation?" "Your servants are shepherds," they replied to Pharaoh, "just as our fathers were." They also said to him, "We have come to live here awhile, because the famine is severe in Canaan and your servants' flocks have no pasture. So now, please let your servants settle in Goshen" (Genesis 47:3-4).

Pharaoh said to Joseph, "Your father and your brothers have come to you, and the land of Egypt is before you; settle your father and your brothers in the best part of the land. Let them live in Goshen. And if you know of any among them with special ability, put them in charge of my own livestock (Genesis 47:5-6).

Because of Christ, God flings wide open the whole kingdom, and simply asks that we take its best. –Springs

Pharaoh was most generous! And even more so based on the fact that, "all shepherds [were] detestable to the Egyptians" (Genesis 46:34b, brackets mine)! But as we touched on earlier, this favor wasn't shown on the basis of the family itself, but rather on Joseph. "Pharaoh knew not these men; but he knew Joseph, and nothing was too good for Joseph and every relative of Joseph."[56] A glorious analogy awaits us here! We are joint–heirs with Christ and as heirs to the Kingdom of God, we too are afforded blessings based solely on our relationship to the Son of God.

> We are "joint–heirs with Christ." Because of Christ, God flings wide open the whole kingdom, and simply asks *that we take its best*. Out of famine–into the best that the kingdom affords! Not only that, but rulers of the King's own property! Oh, Lord Jesus, forgive my un–faith! Open my sin–bound, self–centered eyes to the wonder of Thy love. Teach me how to receive more.

[56] Cowman, Charles E. Mrs., *Springs in the Valley*. pg. 281. Zondervan Publishing House: Grand Rapids MI., 1997, Kindle Version.

The best of the kingdom: that means *Thee*. I take Thee, Lord, as my feast of Eternal Life.[57]

Remember, my sister, our faith has substance! There is something behind it! It's not a faith that simply hopes what we believe God says is true, but rather it knows Him to be true! And if we struggle believing that the whole kingdom of God is ours for the asking, based upon our relationship to Christ, then let us all pray, "Lord! Help us overcome our unbelief!" (Mark 9:24). If we are experiencing a famine of any sorts, then we have the right, as daughters of the King, to petition Him to lead us to a land flowing with milk and honey. That will inevitably look different for all of us, but whether our famine is physical, material, or spiritual, we are offered an audience with the King to ask Him whatever we wish. And since I have learned, through much heartache, that His ways are better and His thoughts so much higher, when I ask anything, I also say, "Your will be done." I want His will more than I even want to get out of my famines since I know those famines are often the times He uses most to strengthen my faith and my character.

"Lord! Help us overcome our unbelief..."

And since I have learned, through much heartache, that His ways are better and His thoughts so much higher, when I ask anything, I also say, "Your will be done."

What about you? Are you experiencing a famine of sorts? Envision yourself standing before the throne of your King. What would you ask?

I heard someone say that the most unused power in the world is the power of the Holy Spirit. If we would only call upon the Lord in faith! The Holy Spirit within us would supply us with all the strength that we need to encounter the tasks set before us. He would empower us to wait upon the Lord for His answers and even give us His peace as we wait. So whatever you have asked of the Lord today, pray they were in accordance with His will and then ask the Lord to fill you to full measure with the Holy Spirit as you wait upon Him for His answer to your needs.

After a long awaited moment, Joseph finally brought his beloved father before Pharaoh. I can imagine the love shared between the reunited father and son as they stood there could nearly be visibly seen by all those in the great hall of Pharaoh's palace. Jacob wasted no time in greeting Pharaoh with a blessing, establishing, just as Joseph once did upon his first encounter with Pharaoh, that the Lord God was his foundation (Genesis 47:7).

After the blessing, what did Pharaoh ask Jacob (47: 8)?

Being a woman, I immediately would have thought, "Why in the world would he ask that? Do I really look that old?" On the contrary, Jacob likely thought nothing of it since he was eager to not only tell his age but rather expound a bit on his pilgrimage as well.

Pharaoh asked him, "How old are you?" Genesis 47:8

And Jacob said to Pharaoh, "The years of my pilgrimage are a hundred and thirty. My years have been few and difficult, and they do not equal the years of the pilgrimage of my fathers." Then Jacob blessed Pharaoh and went out from his presence (Genesis 47:9-10).

Few and difficult? Difficult, yes, but for us to comprehend in our era that his years were few is challenging! And yet, he was right in saying that his years did not equal his father, Isaac, who lived to be one hundred eighty years old and his grandfather, Abraham, who lived to be one hundred seventy–five years old (Genesis 25:7, 35:8). Still, Jacob had

[57] Cowman, Charles E. Mrs., *Springs in the Valley*. pg. 281. Zondervan Publishing House: Grand Rapids MI., 1997, Kindle Version.

lived many years and I think even he would agree that these final years in Goshen were to be his best years yet! "Jacob lived in Egypt seventeen years, and the years of his life were a hundred and forty–seven" (Genesis 47:28).

As the seven years of famine pressed on, the signs of starvation had begun to leave their mark. Yet, due to Joseph's skillful planning in those seven years of abundance, there were still some reserves of grain even toward the end of the seven drought–stricken ones.

Read Genesis 47:13-27. What all did the people of Egypt use to buy grain after their money had run out?

At first glance over this passage, it may seem like Joseph was being somewhat harsh to the people, taking just about everything they had and even reducing them to servitude (47:21). But F.B. Meyer makes a very important point when considering the positive long–term effects of Joseph's decision for the people of Egypt.

> "Then Joseph opened all the storehouses and sold unto the Egyptians." This was right and wise. It would have been a great mistake to give. In the Irish famine the government set the people to earn their bread by making the roads, since it would have done them lasting injury to have allowed them to receive help without rendering some kind of equivalent. And it is not too much to say that it would have taken the Egyptians one or two generations to recover their moral tone if, instead of selling, Joseph had given the grain. Joseph's policy was in exact accord with the maxims of modern political economy..."Why should we die? Buy us and our land for bread." In other words, they became Pharaoh's tenant farmers and paid him twenty percent, or one–fifth of their returns, as rent. This may seem like a heavy tax, but it is not heavier than the levy in most every European country in the present day.[58]

Joseph was not only thinking of the people of Egypt, but also of the country itself from a moral, political standpoint.

Joseph was not only thinking of the people of Egypt, but also of the country itself from a moral and political standpoint. I won't pretend to know politics myself, but I do trust that Joseph was led by the Spirit of God in his actions and that up to this point, his generosity and care for the people was evident in his efforts to provide for them. Joseph was also trying to maintain a strong work ethic among the people so that when the famine was over, families could still thrive and survive. The same implications to a degree can be said of our country as well. Meyer, who lived back in the early nineteen hundreds, was referencing the Irish famine and also European taxes, but we in America experience economic downfalls and also are required to pay taxes. James Sinegal, a co–founder of Costco said, "[If] you don't have a very motivated working class, it starts to affect the dynamics of the economy. If workers are disenchanted and disenfranchised, productivity losses will go along with that."[59] Again, Joseph was looking toward the future, seeing the need for a generation of men and even women to maintain a healthy work ethic for the future generations and economies.

Meanwhile, God remained faithful in His overall provision for Israel.

Now the Israelites settled in Egypt in the region of Goshen. They acquired property there and were fruitful and increased greatly in number (Genesis 47:27).

---

[58] Meyer, F.B. *Joseph, Beloved, Hated, Exalted.* pg. 98, CLC Publications: Fort Washington, PA, 2013.
[59] *Reasons for Optimism: The Results of the 2012 American Time Use Survey*. Laura Stack, The Productivity Pro. July 26, 2013. Theproductivitypro.com.

Let's read the last few verses in today's lesson in Genesis 47:28-31. What did Jacob want Joseph to do for him?

Jacob was finally nearing the end of his time in Goshen with Joseph. Seventeen years probably seemed like seventeen days as the joyous time spent together passed all too quickly. I am at a stage with my girls right now where I want time to stand still and I want them to stay the age and stage they are in! I wish I could bottle it up to keep it forever. Goodness, it makes me cry just thinking about it! You know that's how Jacob and Joseph must have felt. But the biological clock kept ticking and as Jacob was in his final years, he made Joseph swear to him that he would not bury him in Egypt but rather, take him back to Canaan, where his fathers were buried. Jacob made Joseph not only say he would follow through with that request but he also had him do something that probably seems a little strange to us. "...put your hand under my thigh and promise you will show me kindness and faithfulness" (47:29b). Adam Clarke, in his commentary, gives us a great rendering of the meaning of this gesture. "This was a customary manner of taking a solemn oath. The gesture was a reference to the mark of circumcision, the sign of God's covenant, which is equivalent to our laying our hand upon the Bible."[60] I don't know about you, but I think we should stick to laying our hand upon the Bible in courtrooms and at presidential inaugurations. Things might get a little strange if we still used the "hand under thigh" method of taking oaths! But even in the strangeness of the act, the meaning was well understood by both father and son. Such to the degree that Jacob (Israel) was able to bow down at the head of his bed and worship, knowing that Joseph could be trusted long after his passing (47:31, NASB). In tomorrow's lesson we will say goodbye to a beloved father, but before we end, let me ask you a couple more questions.

Seventeen years probably seemed like seventeen days as the joyous time spent together passed all too quickly.

If you were to die today, would there be anything left unreconciled in your life? A relationship perhaps? If so, pray and ask the Lord how He would lead you to reconciliation so that with whatever time you have left on this earth, you will have sought to make right any misunderstandings as best you can. Life is short and we simply cannot bottle up the seasons, no matter how hard we try. The clock is ticking, are we making the most of our time?

[60] *NIV Comparative Study Bible*, footnote. (Adam Clarke, *The Holy Bible with A Commentary*). pg 134. Zondervan, Grand Rapids, MI: 1999.

Day Four: Blessings and Bereavement

People die in one of two ways, either suddenly without any warning, or slowly enough to say goodbye. I have experienced both with two dear family members that I still love to this day with all my heart; my mother and my younger brother. I am sure you too have lost loved ones in either one, or both of these ways. Saying goodbye is so hard, but so is not saying goodbye. Today we get to see how Jacob, also known as Israel, carefully took his time in saying goodbye, to his family, especially his sons. There was enough time for him to not only say goodbye but also to bless each one in a Spirit–inspired way. These blessings carried out prophetically in their lives and the lives of those after them. Since we have two chapters to cover today, we will waste no time digging into our text. But with that said, we also will have to touch lighter on some things more than others. So I am looking to you to be a diligent student with me today and make a point to read carefully the chapters set before us so that we don't miss anything. Now that I have likely scared and overwhelmed you, let's dig in! I promise, we won't read it all at once.

Try to visualize the scene set before us as you read Genesis 48:1-11. In your own words, briefly describe what you envision taking place in these verses.

Tears stream down my face as I read these verses.

Tears stream down my face as I read these verses. Such tenderness and love displayed from the heart of a man whose years, to him, were few and difficult. With failing eyes and yet a thriving soul, Jacob "rallied his strength and sat up in bed" (48:2b). The joy of knowing Joseph had come into his room gave him the strength he needed to give the most precious gift he could give to his beloved son and grandsons. The gift of God's blessing. Notice how he first pondered the faithfulness of God and yet also was reminded of the bitter sting of sorrow that never left his heart: the death of his beloved Rachel (48:7). Here was a man who received the ultimate promise of God Almighty to become a great nation, as did his father and grandfather before him, a man who was given visions and dreams, even wrestled with the pre–incarnate Christ Himself! Can you even imagine what it must have been like for a man like that to reflect on his life as a whole in those precious moments? And Joseph stood there, hanging on every word spoken by his father. His two treasured sons, Manasseh and Ephraim, were standing just a few steps behind him as Jacob got a glimpse of their silhouettes and asked, "Who are these" (48:8)?

"They are the sons God has given me here," Joseph said to his father. Then Israel said, "Bring them to me so that I may bless them." Now Israel's eyes were failing because of old age, and he could hardly see. So Joseph brought his sons close to him, and his father kissed them and embraced them. Israel said to Joseph, "I never expected to see your face again, and now God has allowed me to see your children too (Genesis 48:9-11).

Is that not just like God? We expect so little and yet He delivers so much!

Oh, my heart! There could not have been a dry eye in the room! Is that not just like God? We expect so little and yet He delivers so much! Jacob had already reckoned Joseph's sons as his own. "...Ephraim and Manasseh will be mine, just as Reuben and Simeon are mine" (48:5b). Therefore as the grandsons crawled and sat upon their grandfather's knee,

he held them as if they were his very own sons. Then Joseph, seeing the strength of his father failing, removed the boys from his knee, and "bowed down with his face to the ground," which was a sign of the utmost respect and reverence (48:12).

Read Genesis 48:12-20. Between the boys, to whom did Jacob give the greater blessing?

God acts independently of the claims of priority based on time of birth when He chooses men.

Joseph was not happy about that! Jacob crossed his hands, placing his left hand [considered the lesser] on Manasseh [who was the oldest] and his right hand [considered the greater] on Ephraim [who was the youngest].

> God acts independently of the claims of priority based on time of birth when He chooses men. He too "crossed His hands" in case of Seth whom He chose over Cain; of Shem over Japheth; of Isaac over Ishmael; of Jacob over Esau; of Judah and Joseph over Reuben; of Moses over Aaron; of David over all his brothers; and of Mary of Martha.[61]

Joseph, at the time, did not realize that this was not only the preference of his father Jacob, but rather a prophecy of divine inspiration pointing toward the formation of Ephraim and Manasseh as future tribes.

> This prophecy begins to be fulfilled "from the days of the judges onward, as the tribe of Ephraim in power and compass so increased that is became the head of the northern ten tribes, and its name became of like significance with that of Israel; although in the times of Moses, Manasseh still outnumbered Ephraim by 20,000" (Karl F. Keil and F Delitzsch, Biblical Commentary on the Old Testament). Joshua, whom Israel so long regarded as their ruler, was an Ephraimite. The ark of the covenant was placed in Shiloh in the territory of Ephraim, which increased the tribe's prestige. How could Jacob have prophesied Ephraim's supremacy so positively except by divine inspiration?[62]

Jacob was truly giving the blessings of the Lord upon his deathbed, not of his own will, but of the will of the Father.

Jacob was truly giving the blessings of the Lord upon his deathbed, not of his own will, but of the will of the Father. Notice as he blessed Joseph and his sons, he again reflected on God's faithfulness.

What touches your heart about the blessing Jacob spoke over Joseph and the boys in Genesis 48:15-16?

I think my favorite part of these verses beautifully depicted in the Amplified Bible.

...God [Himself], before Whom my fathers Abraham and Isaac lived and walked before habitually, God [Himself], Who has [been my Shepherd and has led and] fed me from the time I came into being until this day. The redeeming Angel [that is, the Angel the Redeemer–not a created being but the Lord Himself] Who has redeemed me continually from evil, bless the lads! (Genesis 48:15-16a, Amplified Bible).

By faith Jacob, when he was dying, blessed each of Joseph's sons, and worshiped as he leaned on top of his staff. Hebrews 11:21

---

[61] *NIV Comparative Study Bible*, footnote. pg 134. Zondervan, Grand Rapids, MI: 1999.
[62] *NIV Comparative Study Bible*, footnote. (*Karl F. Keil and F Delitzsch, Biblical Commentary on the Old Testament*). pg 136. Zondervan, Grand Rapids, MI: 1999.

There is something so profound and gloriously autonomous in the phrase, "God [Himself]!" To me it means, no one other than God alone could have done all He has done in my life! If anyone realized this to the core of his being, it was Jacob. He had not only experienced God Himself, but had seen God Himself and wrestled with "the Angel the Redeemer–not a created being but the Lord Himself…" (see also Genesis 32:22-32).

Even when we are down and out, we need to look back and ponder the faithfulness of God.

What about you? Can you, like Jacob, say that no one other than God alone could have done all He has done in your life up to this point?

Oh, sister, we have so much to be thankful for! Even when we are down and out, we need to look back and ponder the faithfulness of God. It will remind us that He is always working and will continue to work all things together for our good.

Before Jacob continues the blessings to all of his sons, he made sure to give a certain piece of land to Joseph (48:22). This piece of land would remain as an inheritance to Joseph's descendants long after his death. It would also be the burial place for Joseph's bones (see Joshua 24:32). And one day, even the King of Kings would rest beside a well on this plot of ground in Samaria and give the gift of eternal life to a desperate woman (see John 4:4-5).

Since the blessings that Jacob gave to his sons are filled with prophecy and a depth that we simply cannot unearth in today's lesson, we are going to focus on two of the most important ones.

However, I would still love for you to read Genesis 49:1-28, while underlining and giving special attention to both Judah's and Joseph's blessings (49:8-12, 22-26).

Previously studying the behavior of Joseph's brothers, you may have been able to tell why Jacob spoke some of the things over them as he did. Even though I wish we could study all the blessings in–depth, Judah is worth our time today because we see a great fulfilling of his prophetic blessing, which still continues throughout the ages.

He founded the royal tribe that gave Israel their kings, some of whom were godly leaders, and that ultimately brought Jesus Christ into the world (Heb. 7:14).

> The name of Judah and the Hebrew word for "praise" are very similar (29:35), and Judah did live up to his name. He founded the royal tribe that gave Israel their kings, some of whom were godly leaders, and that ultimately brought Jesus Christ into the world (Heb. 7:14). Judah was a conquering tribe and ruling tribe, and it stayed faithful to the Davidic line when the nation divided. The name "Shiloh" in verse 10 has given rise to many interpretations and speculations, but the most reasonable is that it refers to the Messiah (Num. 24:17). The phrase could be translated "until He comes whose right it is [the scepter, i.e., the rule]," because the word Shiloh means "whose it is." The ancient rabbinical scholars took Shiloh to be a name of the promised Messiah, who alone had the right to claim rule over God's people Israel. The description in verses 11–12 certainly goes beyond Judah's time and speaks of the blessings of the kingdom age when the Messiah shall reign over Israel. Nobody in Old Testament times would use a choice vine for a hitching post for his donkey, because such an act would certainly ruin the vine and probably cause the loss of the animal. Nor would a man's wife waste their precious wine by washing clothes in it! This is the language of hyperbole. It describes a land so

wealthy and a people so prosperous that they can do these outrageous things and not have to worry about the consequences. During the Kingdom Age, when the Messiah reigns, people will enjoy health and beauty (v. 12), because the devastating enemies of human life will be removed.[63]

I hope you enjoyed reading Warren Wiersbe's Bible commentary about the significance of Judah's prophetic blessing as much as I did! God's Word never ceases to astound me with its authenticity and flawless prophetic beauty. Go back over the commentary and underline things that stuck out to you. Isn't it amazing that Jacob gave Judah a blessing that even reaches into the Kingdom Age still to come! Oh goodness, if Jacob had only known the power being spoken through him in those fleeting moments!

Now let's turn our attention to Joseph's blessing. There could be a whole study written on his blessing alone! Since great theologians and Biblical historians can profoundly enlighten us on the prophetical impact of Joseph's blessings, as did Wiersbe with Judah, we will consult the late theologian, John Phillips, with his writings on Joseph. Underline, make notes in the margin, and revel in the authenticity of prophecy within this blessing!

Joseph is a fruitful vine, a fruitful vine near a spring, whose branches climb over a wall. Genesis 49:22

What He Revealed (Genesis 49:22)

The first part of this prophecy has to do with the first coming of Christ. Jacob had his eye on Joseph; the Holy Spirit had his eye on Jesus. And the Holy Spirit was in control throughout the imparting of the blessing. The first part of the prophetic blessing sets before us the virtuous life, the violent death, and the victorious resurrection of Christ. "Joseph is a fruitful bough, even a fruitful bough by a well; whose branches run over a wall" (Gen. 49:22)... The one thing that characterizes a bough is its utter dependence on the tree from which it grows. Jesus was a fruitful bough... Jesus proclaimed His dependence on His Father in heaven...The Lord Jesus also revealed His dependability. He was not only a bough, He was a fruitful bough...He healed the sick, cleansed the leper, and raised the dead..."Joseph is a fruitful bough, even a fruitful bough by a well." The secret of Joseph's astoundingly successful life was that he dwelt by "a well." That is to say, he had hidden resources. Early in his life, he put his roots deep down into the promises of God...Jesus was able to give living water to the woman of Samaria because He dwelt by a well. His roots went deep into the water of the Word of God and into the wellspring of the Spirit of God...[64]

He [Jesus] was not only a bough, He was a fruitful bough...He healed the sick, cleansed the leper, and raised the dead... –Phillips

Whom He Reached

In Genesis 49:22, Jacob spoke not only of a well but of a wall too. Joseph's branches ran over that wall. That wall marked his boundaries as a boy. By the time he was a man, he was far too big to be held within the narrow compass of his home. He reached out–and he ended up ministering to the world, "all countries came into Egypt to Joseph for to buy corn" (Gen. 47:57). In regard to the wall, Jacob spoke of Joseph. The Holy Spirit spoke of Jesus. For Christ's

In regard to the wall, Jacob spoke of Joseph. The Holy Spirit spoke of Jesus. –Phillips

[63] Wiersbe, Warren. *The Wiersbe Bible Commentary*. pg. 137. David C. Cook, Colorado Springs, CO., 2007.
[64] Phillips, John. *Exploring People of the Old Testament*. pg. 186-187. Kregal Publications, Grand Rapids, MI: 2006.

branches, too, also ran over the wall and reached out to the ends of the known world.[65]

How They Hurt Him (Genesis 49:23)

With bitterness archers attacked him; they shot at him with hostility. Genesis 49:23

Joseph's brothers had planned to harm him and would have killed him. Instead they callously sold him to a band of slavers. Jacob's words go far beyond Joseph. They directed our thoughts on Jesus. He too was "grieved" and "shot at." They actually did take up stones as missiles to throw at Him (John 8:59; 10:31). They attacked Him verbally and physically. The leaders of Israel were described by Jacob as "archers." An archer shoots at his enemy. He does not kill him in a hand-to-hand encounter but stands back and accomplishes his purposes from a distance. The Jews let Pilate have the opprobrium of sentencing Jesus to death by crucifixion, but it was the Jewish "archers" who really killed Him.[66]

The Lord's Irresistible Power (Genesis 49:24)

But his bow remained steady, his strong arms stayed limber, because of the hand of the Mighty One of Jacob, because of the Shepherd, the Rock of Israel...Genesis 49:24

"His bow abode in strength." Thus the Lord could say, "No man taketh [my life] from Me, but I lay it down of Myself. I have the power to lay it down, and I have the power to take it again. The Lord's victorious resurrection...the plan, worked out in a past eternity, could not fail; the gates of hell could not prevail against it. Foretelling that twofold plan, Jacob cried, "Thence is the shepherd, the stone of Israel." The Lord was to be the Shepherd and the Stone. Down through the centuries, the Good Shepherd has been minding His flock, multiplying His flock, and gradually moving His flock to the other side. "The stone" points us to His redemptive work for the children of Israel (1 Peter 2:5–12).[67]

Christ's Victory... (Genesis 49:25)

....because of your father's God, who helps you, because of the Almighty, who blesses you with blessings above, blessings of the deep that lies below, blessings of the breast and womb. Genesis 49:25

This verse contains a threefold blessing–a threefold happiness–for Him. Christ's victory in heaven above...In heaven, every knee has already bowed. In hell beneath...Jacob spoke of the "Blessings of the deep that lieth under," and when Jesus died on Calvary's cross, He descended into the deepest halls of hades where He proclaimed His triumph....Christ's victory down here below...Jacob spoke of "blessings of the breasts, and of the womb." The allusion seems to be millennial, for Jesus is yet to reign upon this earth, in the scene of His rejection. He is yet to bring about that golden age of peace and plenty so often hymned by the prophets.[68]

The Eternal Father (Genesis 49:26)

Your father's blessings are greater than the blessings of ancient mountains, than the bounty of age–old hills. Let all these rest on the head of Joseph, on the brow of the prince among his brothers. Genesis 49:26

The mountains will grow old, decay, and crumble, but the blessing Jacob foresaw would last forever...In that human father and son, we see a shadow of the heavenly Father and His beloved Son. With the human Joseph, it is the mighty blessing of Jacob that is in view; with the heavenly Joseph, it is the

---

[65] Ibid, pg. 188.
[66] Ibid, pg. 189.
[67] Ibid, pg. 190-191.
[68] Ibid, pg. 192-193.

> blessing of the heavenly Father in view. "Unto the utmost bound of everlasting hills: they shall be on the head of Joseph, and on the crown of the head of him that was separate ['set apart' or 'the consecrated one'] from the brethren" (Gen. 49:26). Jacob was saying, in other words, that in the eternal state, there would be no end to the prospect or the praise.[69]

He is not done, oh no, our Sovereign, Triune, All–Powerful God is not done yet! Hallelujah!

I can hardly even contain myself after meditating on such glorious revelation foretold from the lips of Jacob on his deathbed! I had to stop several times and just sit in awe of God's plan, which He set in motion from the beginning of time for all humanity. Oh sister, we are a very small part of a very big whole! Christ will bring EVERYTHNG written in Scripture and beyond to full completion. He is not done, oh no, our Sovereign, Triune, and All–Powerful God is not done yet! Hallelujah! And yes, I have the chills as we speak!

Day Five: An Eternal Legacy

After five weeks and soon to be twenty–five days of homework, I believe we still have merely scratched the surface to the depths of significance of Joseph's life! Even he could NEVER have imagined how his faithful obedience to God would magnificently impact eternity. If nothing else, his life ought to make us thrive with the desire to live a life in obedience to Christ and persevere even under the direst of circumstances that come our way. We attempted to sum up one–hundred and ten years of the life of a man who clothed himself with integrity and resolved to live in purity. At best, ladies, we have ninety years, a few more or a few less. How are we going to resolve to live it from this day forward? I want to live it like Joseph. What about you?

If nothing else, his life ought to make us thrive with a desire to live a life in obedience to Christ and persevere even under the direst of circumstances that come our way.

From our teaching lessons to homework lessons, if you could pick one thing that struck you so deeply from the life of Joseph, what would it be?

It is almost impossible for me to answer the question I asked you to just answer! Seems fair, right! That's because where you have spent five weeks, I have spent years with Joseph and he has been on my mind almost daily. I cannot tell you how many times I envisioned his birth, life, and death with vivid color and imagery. And since there are still so many missing pieces, I'll just have to wait until heaven to sit down with him and ask him to share his testimony with me! Oh, and believe me, he's not the only one I'll be hunting down for details! We have so much to look forward to. It's going to take eternity just to sit with all of those who have gone before us and hear their testimonies. Won't that be glorious!

And since there are still so may missing pieces, I'll just have to wait until heaven to sit down with him and ask him to share his testimony with me!

But as we bring our feet back to the dirt floor of Jacob's tent, today we must say goodbye, not only to our faithful patriarch, but also his beloved son. And await the reunion, seeing them with our own eyes together one day in glory!

---

[69]Ibid, pg. 194-195.

Placing yourself as best you can in Joseph's sandals, read Genesis 49:29-33 & 50:1.

As the dry, cracked, weather–worn feet attached to his earthly shell were drawn up from the floor where he sat into his straw sheep's wool bed, Jacob took one last look at his beloved Joseph, inhaled his last breath of Egypt's thick desert air, and "was gathered to his people" (Genesis 49:33b). And just as a young boy clinging to the strong arms of a father, "Joseph threw himself upon his father and wept over him and kissed him" (Genesis 50:1). The hundred and forty–seven year old vessel, finally shut down, placed on hold in the "cave in the field of Machpelah, near Mamre in Canaan" until that glorious day of the resurrection of the body (Genesis 49:30, see also 1 Cor. 15:35-44)!

Then Joseph directed the physicians in his service to embalm his father Israel. So the physicians embalmed him, taking a full forty days, for that was the time required for embalming. And the Egyptians mourned for him seventy days. Genesis 50:2-3

As was Egyptian custom, Joseph requested that his father be embalmed by the physicians in his service. Such a process took "a full forty days" and not only did his family mourn for him, but so did the Egyptians, for seventy days (Genesis 50:2-3)! Jacob's embalming, or the preservation of his body, was also a beautiful parallel of the way that Egypt would preserve the nation of Israel until their Exodus back to Canaan. And note that the Lord had already used Egypt to provide for His people, preserving them through a famine that threatened to wipe them out entirely.

Briefly describe the elaborate funeral that was held for Jacob as you read Genesis 50:4-14.

"...The Egyptians are holding a solemn ceremony of mourning." That is why that place near the Jordan is called Abel Mizraim [mourning of the Egyptians]. Genesis 50:11b

As we touched on before, one of the reasons that "all Pharaoh's officials accompanied him [Joseph] –the dignitaries of his court and all the dignitaries of Egypt..." to hold such an elaborate ceremony for Jacob, was due to Joseph's grand position in Egypt (50:7, brackets mine). Lamenting "loudly and bitterly," all those in attendance, including the members of Joseph's household, his brothers and those belonging to his father's household, mourned for seven days by a threshing floor near the Jordan River (50:8, 10). Now imagine all those in attendance, the "great cloud of witnesses" in the heavens above, the angels, and on the earth below, Jews, Gentiles, people from all nations who had gathered for the Passover, mourning at the death of our Savior! Even those who had never known Him felt the sorrow and weight of His death on the Cross (Heb. 12:1, Matt. 26:17). Little did all those in attendance know of the forgiveness and grace that would be extended to them and to all humanity upon His resurrection!

After the funeral, grief quickly turned to fear for Joseph's brothers who themselves were hoping that the forgiveness once extended, would remain forever.

When their message came to him, Joseph wept. Genesis 50:17b

When Joseph's brothers saw that their father was dead, they said, "What if Joseph holds a grudge against us and pays us back for all the wrongs we did to him?" So they sent word to Joseph, saying, "Your father left these instructions before he died: 'This is what you are to say to Joseph: I ask you to forgive your brothers the sins and the wrongs they committed in treating you so badly.' Now please forgive the sins of the servant of the God of your father." When their message came to him, Joseph wept (Genesis 50:15-17).

Have you ever forgiven someone for a wrong they committed against you, but had to reassure them of that forgiveness at a later time? Or vice versa, where you needed reassuring, upon a change of events, that the forgiveness once extended to you would remain? Briefly explain.

Forgiveness is so much more than mere words. We communicate it through our actions, our reactions, the tone of our voice, the compassion in our hearts, and by the complete riddance of any sort of grudge held against the one whom we seek to genuinely forgive. I imagine that Joseph never once gave his brothers any reason, by his actions, to doubt his forgiveness toward them, which he showed back in Genesis 45, when revealing his identity to them. In fact, I think it's safe to say that all his actions, the lavish provisions, the food and the land all proved the way he felt toward his brothers and the whole family. However, F.B. Meyer, said, "…it would appear that, for a long time, his brothers, judging of him by their own dark and implacable hearts, could not believe in the sincerity and genuineness of his forgiveness."[70]

I imagine that Joseph never once gave his brothers any reason, by his actions, to doubt his forgiveness toward them...

Do you ever find it hard to accept the forgiveness given to you through salvation in Jesus Christ? Do you ever feel like maybe the things you have done in your past are just too terrible to have genuinely forgiven?

Listen, my dear sister, the price paid on the cross for your sin and my sin was expensive! If Jesus blood made atonement for all the sins of the world, past, present, and future, then it is more than enough to cover even your deepest, darkest, most painful sin (see John 3:16, 13:1). Jesus can forgive you completely, even if you cannot forgive yourself. If you struggle with this, pray that God will help you to fully believe and trust His forgiveness. The more you believe He has forgiven you [which is the most important thing], the easier it will be to forgive yourself. I have heard many women say, "But I just don't feel forgiven." And to that I have always said, based on my own experience, believe the truth first and the feeling will come later. Just as Joseph wept, I believe Jesus also weeps when we, judging by our "own dark and implacable hearts," do not "believe the sincerity and genuineness of His forgiveness" to us. Oh, sister, He can carry the weight of your sin! He can remove the guilt and shame that goes with it, if you will let Him. And just as Joseph's brothers came to him and threw themselves down before him, saying, "We are your slaves," we too can throw ourselves at the feet of Jesus (Genesis 50:18)! We can become His slave, a slave to righteousness and no longer a slave to sin (see Romans 6:18)!

Jesus can forgive you completely, even if you cannot forgive yourself.

We can become His slave, a slave to righteousness and no longer a slave to sin...

With reassurance, compassion, and tenderness, Joseph responded to his anxious brother's message.

But Joseph said to them, "Don't be afraid. Am I in the place of God? You intended to harm me, but God intended it for good to accomplish what is now being done, the saving of many lives. So then, don't be afraid. I will provide for you and your children." And he reassured them and spoke kindly to them (Genesis 50:19-20).

"The forgiveness might well be amazing to these men because it was *not of this world at all,*" says Meyer.[71] Joseph understood, as the Amplified Bible states, "[Vengeance is His, not mine.], when he said, "Am I in the place of God" (50:19)? Only the eyes and a heart of faith could leave oneself completely in the hands of an all–knowing, all–wise, and all–powerful God! And that is exactly what Joseph did. He saw past the pain of his former years and by doing so was able to praise God for His perfect plan. How deeply

He saw past the pain of his former years and by doing so was able to praise God for His perfect plan.

[70] Meyer, F.B. *Joseph, Beloved, Hated, Exalted.* pg. 150, CLC Publications: Fort Washington, PA, 2013, Kindle Version.
[71] Ibid, pg. 151.

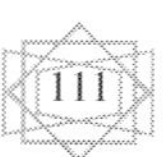

...You have been faithful with a few things; I will put you in charge of many things...Matthew 25:21

*For **if you forgive** people their trespasses [their reckless and willful sins, leaving them, letting them go, and giving up resentment], your heavenly Father will also forgive you. **But if you do not forgive** others their trespasses [their reckless and willful sins, letting them go, and giving up resentment], neither will your Father forgive you your trespasses. Matthew 6:14-15 (Amplified Bible, emphasis mine)*

Joseph's legacy and life of obedience lived on throughout many generations and still does today.

...But God will surely come to your aid...

and powerfully this truth can speak to us, ladies! No matter what situation you are in right now, if your heart is set on following God's ways, His will, and walking close to Him, He will use it for your good and quite possibly for the "saving of many lives." Joseph remained faithful in the small things as a slave, in the challenging things as a prisoner, and in the things of utmost importance as the governor of Egypt. He couldn't see what God was doing then, but he chose to "live by faith and not by sight" and standing before his brothers again, saw the plan fully executed as God had foreordained it (2 Cor. 5:7). It was because of this life of faith in the Lord and not in his brothers, or anyone else for that matter, that he was able to forgive. He removed himself from the situation entirely and focused on God. He allowed the Spirit of God to dwell in him so richly that forgiveness came to him as his gift to give away. However, more than a gift, it was also an act of obedience to God.

What did Jesus say about forgiveness in Matthew 6:14-15?

According to Jesus, harboring resentment and unforgiveness is a serious issue that must be dealt with! We will not experience peace, joy, or genuine rest for our souls, maybe even physical rest, if we are harboring bitterness toward someone. Even if the one who offended you does not seek your forgiveness, you must go to God and plead with Him to help you let go and give up your resentment. The feelings of bitterness may take a while to subside, but you can stand on God's truth and trust Him to override those feelings with time and commitment to obedience. Holding onto our grudge is simply not worth it! There is more at stake than we realize! It will affect generations long after us if we do not settle it now and therefore break the cycle of unforgiveness.

Joseph's legacy and life of obedience lived on throughout many generations and still does today. He was blessed by God to not only see his grandchildren, but his great grandchildren as well!

Joseph stayed in Egypt, along with his father's family. He lived a hundred and ten years and saw the third generation of Ephraim's children. Also the children of Makir son of Manasseh were placed at birth on Joseph's knees (Genesis 50:22-23).

And as the life of a legend began to come to an end, Joseph gave specific instructions to his brothers. At that point, I am not certain which brothers were still living, since many of them were much older than Joseph, but whoever was in attendance, they were given very specific orders.

*Then Joseph said to his brothers, "I am about to die. **But God will surely come to your aid** and take you up out of this land to the land He promised on oath to Abraham, Isaac and Jacob." And Joseph made the sons of Israel swear an oath and said, "God will surely come to your aid, and then you must carry my bones up from this place (Genesis 50:24-25, emphasis mine).*

F.B. Meyer makes an important comparison between Jacob's dying wish and Joseph's that is worth us reading!

> Let us investigate the full importance of these words. And we may do so best by comparing them with Jacob's dying wish: "Bury me with my fathers in the cave that is in the field of Machpelah." This was most natural: we all love to be

> buried by the beloved dust of our departed. And Jacob knew that there would be no great difficulty in carrying out his request. Joseph was then in the plentitude of his power; there was no great faith involved, therefore in asking for that which could so easily be accomplished. But with Joseph it was different. He, too, wanted to be buried in the land of Canaan; but not at once, not then! There were two things he expected would happen: the one, that the people would go out of Egypt; the other, that they would come into the land of Canaan. He did not know when or how; he was only sure that it would be: "surely."[72]

Like Jacob, Joseph's dying wish held within it a greater prophetic meaning than he could have ever imagined!

Like Jacob, Joseph's dying wish held within it a greater prophetic meaning than he could have ever imagined! Again, a life lived in faith, and now dying in faith! "To Joseph's natural vision these things were most unlikely."[73] And in speaking of Israel being taken back to Canaan by the great Exodus, I love how Meyer says, "He [Joseph] did not know when or how; he was only sure that it would be…" Indicated beautifully as Joseph said, "Surely God will come to your aid…" (50:25b). Just take a minute to saturate your soul in the unabated truth of the promise spoke by the Holy Spirit of God through the mouthpiece of His dying warrior!

Faith, my sister, faith!

What has been left undone in your life up to this point where you need to proclaim in faith that, "Surely God will come to my aid!"

Faith, my sister, faith!

Now faith is being sure of what we hope for and certain of what we do not see. This is what the ancients were commended for... By faith Joseph, when his end was near, spoke about the exodus of the Israelites from Egypt and gave instructions about his bones (Hebrews 11:1, 22).

Everything we believe and everything we live out is by faith!

One day, let it be said of us, "By faith…"

Everything we believe and everything we live out is by faith! Not faith in the outcome, but faith in our God! Oh, to live with our eyes so fixed on Jesus that we accept everything from His hand, passionately seek Him in His Word, and persevere daily in living a life of obedience. Who knows, we may be living our own Joseph legacy and still in the first few chapters! So with all my heart and with tears welling up in my eyes, I pray that when you put down your pen and when you close your Bible, the life of Joseph will be forever before you all your days. I pray that the work we have done will not be in vain, but will change us for all eternity. So until next time, my sweet sister in Christ, know I love you deeply and could not be more proud of you and grateful for our precious time spent in the pages of the Word.

I love you, my sister. Until next time...

---

[72] Meyer, F.B. *Joseph, Beloved, Hated, Exalted.* pg. 152, CLC Publications: Fort Washington, PA, 2013, Kindle Version.
[73] Ibid, 152-153.

LESSON FIVE

The Blessing of the Bones

By faith, Joseph, when his end was near, spoke about the exodus of the Israelites from Egypt and gave instructions about his bones (Hebrews 11:22).

I. Joseph's bones spoke of ____________ ________________.[74]

–*Then Joseph said to his brothers, "I am about to die. But God will surely come to your aid and take you up and out of this land He promised on an oath to Abraham, Isaac and Jacob…then you must carry my bones up from this place" (Gen. 50:24-25).*

–Through salvation in Jesus Christ, we too are promised ______________ from bondage by the power of the Holy Spirit (Is. 61:1 & 2 Cor. 3:17).

II. Joseph's bones spoke of ____________ ________________.[75]

–*Moses took the bones of Joseph with him because Joseph had made the sons of Israel swear an oath…(Exodus 13:19).*

–Moses carried the memorial body of _____________ through his desert and we carry the memorial body of _____________ through ours (Luke 22:19 & 2 Cor. 4:10).

III. Joseph's bones spoke of ____________ ________________.[76]

–*And Joseph's bones, which the Israelites had brought up from Egypt, were buried at Shechem…(Josh. 24:32).*

–"The patriarch's coveted burial in Canaan because they wanted to be in the Promise ___________ when the promised _____________ arrived," says Phillips (Matt. 27:50-53).[77]

– If we are in Christ, death is not our final _________________ (1 Cor. 15:42-44).

---

[74] Phillips, John. *Exploring People of the Old Testament*. pg. 200. Kregal Publications, Grand Rapids, MI: 2006.
[75] Ibid, pg. 204.
[76] Ibid, pg. 205.
[77] Ibid, pg. 204.

GROUP DISCUSSION QUESTIONS

The Blessing of the Bones

1. As he was dying, Joseph believed God would one day free the Israelites from bondage in Egypt. Do you believe God can free you from your seasons of bondage or maybe someone else who you know is going through a difficult time in their lives? How does Joseph's faith in God's deliverance encourage you?

2. Just as Moses carried Joseph's bones in the desert as a reminder of God's promise, how can we be encouraged in difficult times by focusing on Christ's death on the cross and what it means for our salvation?

3. If you had been at the scene of the crucifixion, try to imagine what it must have been like after Jesus died and the graves of the dead burst open!

4. How does the reminder that earth is not our final destination, bring you encouragement in your current circumstances today?

66794308R00066

Made in the USA
Lexington, KY
25 August 2017